Praise for *Quiet Voices*

Vic Matthews is one of the most fertile minds in contemporary biblical scholarship. His capacity to write clearly on the topic of silence in the biblical sources is an outstanding example. Both seasoned scholars and ordinary readers can readily comprehend the richness of the meaning he derives from his use of anthropology to enlighten the biblical texts, how man, woman, and the deity, too, were viewed in the Old Testament in down-to-earth terms. The book's sophistication is of a high order and relayed with a lightness of touch that at every turn makes for stimulating reading.

—Calum Carmichael, emeritus professor of comparative literature and law, Cornell University

Victor Matthews does what he does so well in this book—exploring what is hidden, between the lines, sensed, felt, and in this case unsaid in order to show us the Bible in a new way. Situated within a larger frame of the way silence functions in literature and everyday life, Matthews's work makes a useful and practical companion to Auerbach's famous essay in *Mimesis* ("Odysseus' Scar") for thinking about the strange and artful ways biblical authors speak through the things they do not tell us.

—Brian R. Doak, professor of biblical studies, George Fox University, and author of *Consider Leviathan: Narratives of Nature and the Self in Job*

Silence is often ignored and unappreciated in our noisy world. Biblical interpreters have by and large failed to recognize the literary and theological significance of silence in Scripture. Thankfully, Victor Matthews's study goes a long way in rectifying this as he masterfully shows how the theme of silence contributes to a deeper, more profound understanding of the text and the characters appearing therein. Matthews's insightful analysis of this neglected topic is a fascinating read that I heartily recommend.

—Robert B. Chisholm Jr., chair and senior professor of Old Testament studies, Dallas Theological Seminary

Matthews explores silence in the Old Testament as an art historian might explore darkness in a Caravaggio painting, not simply noticing it but interrogating it. God's "absence" in silence can be purposeful—summoning our attention, offering us peace, calling us to repent, or inviting us to be still and trust God to act when the time is right. It's amazing what the darkness can tell us about the light.

—The Rev. John Spicer, rector, St. Andrew's Episcopal Church, Kansas City, Missouri; author of *Beating the Boundaries: The Church God Is Calling Us to Be*

QUIET VOICES

QUIET VOICES

SILENCE IN THE
HEBREW BIBLE

VICTOR H. MATTHEWS

FORTRESS PRESS
Minneapolis

QUIET VOICES
Silence in the Hebrew Bible

29 28 27 26 25 24   1 2 3 4 5 6 7 8 9

Library of Congress Control Number: 2024938078

Cover design: Kristin Miller
Cover image: Pure lo-fi grainy gradient texture. Violet gradient
background. - stock illustration by olegagafonov/Getty Images

Print ISBN: 979-8-8898-3376-5
eBook ISBN: 979-8-8898-3384-0

To all those who find silence a welcome companion

CONTENTS

PREFACE

In some ways this volume on silence is an extension of my recent book *Experiencing Scripture: The Five Senses in Biblical Interpretation* (Fortress, 2023). I had become intrigued with how the five senses were highlighted in biblical narrative, law, and wisdom, and that meant I explored sound as one of these facets. The flip side of sound is silence. The lack of sound or at least of the sounds we expect to hear is a phenomenon that can reassure as well as frighten us. It adds mystery and a sense of expectation to our lives and has been used for thousands of years by authors and poets who recognized silence's effect on the human mind and psyche. As a result, as I built my research chart of all the instances in the Hebrew Bible that used specific vocabulary or synonyms for silence, I was amazed at how pervasive it was. In fact, I came to realize that silence is an essential factor, driving a narrative forward, shaping the actions of the characters, and creating or sparking emotions.

At the time I was doing my research, I was in my last year as dean of my college and was planning to retire after serving as a university professor for forty-five years. The exercise of searching for Hebrew words and phrases reminded me that there would be life after administrative tasks were put aside. The energy I put into my research, between doing the paperwork and attending meetings, kept me going many days and energized me to look forward to a time when I could do more than just "fit in" my research. It is my hope that you will be just as excited as I was looking for silence in its many forms. I guarantee it is worth the effort.

I would be remiss if I did not give credit to those who have assisted me in this work. First, is Don Benjamin. We have coauthored several works, including the new fifth edition of *Old Testament Parallels: Laws and Stories from the Ancient Near East* (Paulist, 2023). In recent years we have had a habit of exchanging drafts of our individual projects, and I have always benefited from his cogent comments and suggestions. He has been my muse over the years, and I cannot thank him enough for that. In addition, I want to thank Carey Newman, my editor at Fortress Press. He was kind enough to read early drafts of the chapters in *Quiet Voices* and he is responsible for expanding my reading and research into literary studies. Over the years, I have worked with many editors, but Carey is the rare professional who takes the time and interest to ensure a manuscript in the making is transformed into a readable and helpful volume. And, of course, I want to thank all my colleagues and friends who allowed me to buttonhole them in the hallway or listened patiently while I discussed this project or asked about a specific text.

Victor H. Matthews, Emeritus Professor of Religious Studies
Missouri State University
February 2024

CHAPTER ONE

The Sound of Silence

THE SOUND OF silence is a profound experience. It is refreshing, scary, intimidating, and disappointing. When used strategically, it can exclude ideas and persons, and it can also be caring, a form of respect or a demonstration of empathy.[1] In its most positive connotation, silence can be pleasant or soothing, even taking on what we imagine to be a form of heavenly calm. But silence is also ambiguous, wavering between the two extremes of pleasurable and devastating.[2] That may be why we so often describe silence as uncomfortable, awkward, and embarrassing. If silence is ominous, even deathly, it is also an integral part of life and therefore a phenomenon worth a closer look.

When I told a friend I was thinking about writing a book about silence, the first question was, of course, why? What is there to say about silence other than it occurs? Does it really matter, and why would anyone think it would be interesting to study? I responded by saying that everyone has experience with silence in one form or another. Silence occurs between words during conversation, between musical notes in a composition, and serves as an indicator of mood and emotion. It often signals shocking or revealing actions.[3] Silence occurs in a theater or a concert hall just prior to a performance. If it persists too long, however, silence results in perplexity and concern, especially if the lack of response involves someone special or God. There is a real sense of expectancy and anticipation as silence precedes the arrival of the actors, musicians, and backstage staff. Silence is sometimes the most precious commodity in life and the basis for various types of spirituality.[4] Examining silence in the context of the Hebrew Bible gives the reader the opportunity to ask significant questions about why silence occurs, its value to the narrative or the narrator, and how it relates to our understanding of God.

When we engage in conversation, we generally take turns rather than talk over each other. Your silence when I speak may be because you are being attentive and are interested in what I have to say, or it is a sign of deference/politeness rather than interrupting me.[5] There is also the occasional pause (i.e., silence) between words or as part of a conversation in which a person tries to think of just the right word or phrase. It is these small silences that add meaning or emphasis to the conversation. Used correctly, silence serves as vocal punctuation, allowing comprehension to be enhanced. Silence prevents a flood of speech that could overwhelm or mask the meaning of any statement and allows for a reasonable examination of what is being said.[6]

From a functional aspect, silence is a form of avoidance. It is an indication that a certain topic or aspect of a topic will not or cannot be discussed.[7] Remaining silent in this instance is a personal or conscious choice, although one that may have been enforced by someone else or by certain circumstances.[8] Silence can also be a strategy employed by an author to better focus on the theme of a play or story. By limiting what is spoken, closing off what could be an infinite number of cognitive choices, the reader or audience is skillfully directed by the author to a chosen conclusion.[9]

There are some who use silence as they speak to add gravity to what has just been spoken. Political speech often contains significant pauses to allow for applause, to add importance to what has just been said, or to signal the next point to be made.[10] Skilled orators can intimidate another person with a pause and a meaningful look. And, in some cases, silence by an individual whose words are seldom given much credence or weight is considered a good thing.[11] Silence also can serve as a form of punctuation, either adding passion to the discussion or bringing it to an end. As a result, if we were to time the duration of our interactions, there would be a fair amount of silent spacing, hesitation, stuttering, or thoughtful pausing as part of our discussion. What matters is how often and at what point there are silences and how they facilitate or obstruct conversation or the telling of a story.

It is a given that in speech silence demands both a response and interpretation.[12] No silence or nonverbal gesture ever goes unnoticed, and therefore it requires the mind to search for its meaning.[13] On a larger scale, we seldom if ever experience total silence. In fact, it would be startling, even frightening for anyone who is not hearing impaired to experience true soundlessness. There is always background noise—insects buzzing, the wind blowing through the trees, the distant sound of voices or motor vehicles. Although total silence is practically unattainable, the cessation of many of the normal sounds that surround us can be restful and refreshing. Walking through a woodland with only the sounds associated with the movement of animals and perhaps the lapping of water in a stream is sufficiently different to allow for an appreciation of the world in which we live. Plus, crunching leaves under our feet can be a pleasure that we do not often take the time to enjoy. All these sounds that are too seldom experienced give us a chance to think without the distraction of identifying them. And when we cannot escape the normal sounds of modern life (traffic, sirens, the cry of children at play), we have a way of shutting them out by negating their importance and concentrating only on what we want to hear—which is a form of silencing.[14]

Somehow our minds have a built-in register of sounds that are expected in normal circumstances, and when they are not present, we become anxious, frightened, or agitated. We crave normality. That can include a degree of personal silence depending on where you are (at home, in a classroom, or in the library), a particular activity (concert or speech), or situations when you are commanded or expected to remain silent based on age, gender, or social status. But even so, there are sounds occurring all the time. To be silent then becomes a choice, but one that cannot always command others to join in the fun.

One of the principal differences between the oral and written version of a story is that silence is more effective in written narratives. Long pauses and silent characters simply do not work for a live audience. Even when someone reads a story, silence is one of those conditions that may be baffling until its purpose is made clear. When used effectively, silence allows the biblical author the opportunity to fashion and control a story while giving precedence to a dominant narrative voice. It reflects the author's intent and forms the basis for the creation of meaning, both for the author and for the authorial audience.[15] This authorial audience comprises the original as well as later audiences who share the cultural background of the author. Unlike modern readers, they are aware that the story is "made up" and realize that it and its characters are based on what the author has chosen to convey using a well-known story or myth. They know that it is intended to be entertaining or instructive for his or her readers.[16]

Depending on the complexity of the story and the number of characters involved, the reader may be forced to accept a set of conditions like silence being placed on the characters that are outside the normal or everyday forms of human interaction that are comfortable for the audience.[17] The constructed frame or restrictive elements of the story first draw the reader into the world of the story and then introduce a set of characters. Using silence as a narrative strategy in dealing with characters can mean that major and minor characters may remain entirely silent or only speak occasionally. The intentionality or story plan of the author "can only be known insofar as the intention is reproduced in his or her text."[18] There is a basic presupposition that the events in the story reflect the purposes of the author, either consciously or unconsciously, and that way the author creates meaning.

In constructing a narrative, depending on the genre of the text, the author makes decisions on setting, dialogue, and character development. Among these decisions is the degree to which the narrator either attaches dialogue together or controls the recital of the story in progress by a narrator. The characters tend to fade into the background if the decision is made to employ a nameless, anonymous "narrator-arranger . . . who exercises silent control through the ordering [or exclusion] of discourse."[19] They may be on stage, but their movements and the few lines they recite are secondary to the narrator's cues to the audience. For example, in the annals of the kings of Israel and Judah in 1–2 Kings, a scribal narrator is very often the only voice and the reader is dependent on what the scribes choose to include (e.g., the Deuteronomistic historian).[20] The presentation is held to a very rigid style by ideological and scribal convention that creates a chronology of significant happenings but seldom includes dialogue in its abbreviated, stylized recording of events.[21] A similar technique is also used in modern literary works. For instance, Walker Percy's novel *Lancelot* concentrates on the title character, who serves as both the narrator and protagonist and who "controls the flow and content of the material, never checked or refuted."[22] In this instance, the reader's interpretative options are reduced to those being arranged by the narrator.

If a narrator is not overtly present, then the reader-text interaction is freed up to apply a variety of meanings to the story.[23] However, the author can only create "a version of reality whose acceptability is governed by convention and 'narrative necessity' . . . although ironically, we have no compunction about calling stories true or false."[24] In fact, whether a story is considered to be a true account is less important than its entertainment value and the resonance of its theme to the audience.

Components of This Volume

This volume explores the language, context, and purpose of silence in the Hebrew Bible.[25] It traces silence across the Bible's many genres (narrative, law, prophecy, psalmody, and wisdom) by using theoretical frames drawn from various academic disciplines (communication studies, political science, literary criticism, and sociological studies). The book examines how silence is used as a literary technique, particularly by the author and narrator, and how it theologically connects to themes of obedience, grief, hope, personal relationships, trauma, politics, and wisdom. The volume concludes with a theological reflection on the perplexing silence of God in the face of human longing for a response.[26]

The volume is laid out in five parts that build upon an intellectual foundation of studies on the idea and concept of silence. Some of these works will be unfamiliar to those who are used to engaging in biblical studies alone. Some draw on literary techniques, while others are the work of sociologists, anthropologists, political scientists, and psychologists. They are referenced in the footnotes and in the bibliography. Spending time reading through these aids will facilitate those who wish to delve deeper into this subject and will serve as a road map of sources on the subject.

It is my hope that after reading this volume you will also find value in studying or just thinking about how silence fits into all aspects of human culture, into literature, into conversation, and into social dynamics. If nothing else, I challenge you to consider how silence has impacted your own life and those around you. Try silence: you may like it.

CHAPTER TWO

Silent Sacrifice in the Aqedah

IN THE CLASSIC story of the Aqedah (binding of Isaac) in Genesis 22, silence reigns supreme. The common perception is that the story of Abraham's sacrifice of Isaac revolves around these two major characters. However, it is the long stretches of silence that shape the story and its characters and serve as the dominant factor as the story unrolls. The characters are not allowed to exhibit typical human emotions or concerns and very seldom are allowed to speak. Instead, they are portrayed as wooden figures moved about on the board and exhibiting only those characteristics—particularly obedience—that fit into the scheme or design of the omniscient narrator.[1] Thus, a focus on silence as the key to the construction of this story can bring the modern reader and the ancient authorial audience closer together in an appreciation of its artistic development.[2]

Genesis 22 begins with a familiar story theme. Abraham goes on a journey. Well, to be honest, that is the way nearly all the stories about heroes like Abraham begin. Like other heroic characters, Abram/Abraham is constantly being sent on a journey or being forced by environmental forces into making a journey—usually as part of his acceptance or allegiance to the covenant promise made with YHWH. Each step along the way, he and his household establish social, legal, and theological precedents (circumcision, endogamy, YHWH-alone worship). These then become the cultural foundation for traditional practices and beliefs in ancient Israel.

The strategy of silence and the journey motif first appear in the ancestral narratives when Abram's character is introduced in Genesis 12. He silently accompanies his father from Ur of the Chaldees north up the Euphrates River to Haran. After his father's death, perhaps wondering what the future held, God commands Abram to undertake a journey into the unknown. He must leave his extended household and his urban existence in Haran behind in exchange for a promise of land and children. Despite its risks, this would have been an enticing offer since Abram and his wife Sarai are well past childbearing age, and they had few prospects beyond clientage to other family members in Haran.

Unlike the journey recorded in the epic tale of the Mesopotamian hero Gilgamesh, Abram is not entirely self-centered in his quest. Gilgamesh's goal is to obtain the knowledge or the means to avoid his own death.[3] Abram, whose household will be doomed to extinction unless he obtains an heir, is seeking a form of immortality for his household. What is important to his story is that he demonstrates obedience to the will of his patron deity. Abram leaves Haran without asking questions or voicing any of the typical objections that he could have made. His silent acceptance merits him the promised gift of land and children for himself and his descendants.

Silent, unquestioned obedience is the key to Abram's narrative and will become the cardinal characteristic for which he will become known as the eponymous hero and founder of the Israelite people. His actions and his fidelity to YHWH become the standard for the Israelite culture, setting them on the journey to focus their allegiance on YHWH, who called to Abram and made a covenant with him and his descendants.

As he departs from Haran, the only guidance he has is that YHWH has promised to "show" him to the land in question. YHWH supplies no details about the route Abram is to take nor any of the events along the way as he sets out for the land of Canaan (Gen 12:5). The only glimpse provided in the text is the mention of Eliezer of Damascus as his adopted heir (Gen 15:2), giving the audience a clue about the stops during his journey prior to reaching Shechem (12:6). He has no idea what he will find when he gets there, except that the Canaanites already inhabit the land. Still, he departs without making any direct response or attempting to negotiate. His silence, imposed on him by the author, then becomes Abram's most common characteristic throughout most of the rest of the narrative cycle. The question then arises why the author has chosen not to allow characters, major or minor, to speak and instead to rely heavily on a narrator's voice. The answer, as we will see, seems to be that this is a strategic choice.

In this way the author can set aside the norm of continuous communication between characters. Then when it is most appropriate or impactful, the silence is broken. This pattern often occurs in musical compositions or at a crucial moment designed to emphasize a key factor in a story's composition.[4] An intentional gap in dialogue adds to the humor or the tension in a story as the audience waits for the next scene to resume or speculates on why the gap occurs at that point. That strategy is in place throughout most of the cycle of stories in Genesis 12–25. Abram/Abraham remains silent or is a man of very few words. Thus, waiting for Abram/Abraham to speak becomes a standard for the audience, and when he does speak it becomes significant.

For example, Abram only speaks once in Genesis 12 (to Sarai, Gen 12:11–13) when they migrate to Egypt and they must disguise their marital relationship. In the story of Lot's separation from Abram's household, dialogue is also kept to a minimum while they work to ensure that their herds have sufficient grazing areas (13:8–9). The only real exceptions to this rule occur in the two transactional dialogues in Genesis 18:16–33 and 23:2–16, which coincidentally do not involve a journey. They stand out because the narrator's voice is set aside, at least temporarily, and the characters are then allowed to drive the action of the story and for once show some real emotions. Breaking their silence is such a contrast that the importance of the theme in these narratives becomes a heightened narrative feature.

In the first of these examples, conversation centers on a divine decision to destroy Sodom and Gomorrah. Instead of letting this announcement pass, as he so often does, Abraham initiates a legal argument based on the ethical principle of right behavior: "Will you indeed sweep away the righteous with the wicked?" (Gen 18:23). The question, at its heart, centers on whether an ethical deity can retain that label if the god engages in unfair and willful destruction of a people without first determining if there are righteous persons among them. It is almost amusing to see Abraham's careful, almost ritualistic, yet impassioned bargaining with God over the number of righteous persons needed to spare the doomed cities.[5] The polite questioning ends once an acceptable figure of ten righteous persons has been established between them. Abraham then silently returns to his encampment to await the outcome (18:33).

The transactional dialogue in Genesis 23:2–16 follows a similar pattern with Abraham, a resident alien, first addressing the elders of Hebron as a supplicant. He wishes to gain their support before he bargains with Ephron the Hittite, the owner of the property that Abraham wishes to purchase for a burial site for Sarah and his household. Ephron takes advantage of Abraham during their bargaining, boxing him in to offering to pay whatever the owner requested.[6] Abraham's need outweighs his desire for a good or even a fair deal. What is most important is the bill of sale that functions as the foundation for Israel's later claim to the land.[7] Abraham then buries his wife without another word (Gen 23:17–19).

Given these exceptions, why does the author employ a primarily passionless and silent hero in the remainder of the stories? Certainly, the strategy does drive the narrative forward more quickly, allowing the omniscient narrator to focus the readers' attention on a narrower pathway. The choice to withhold a typical dialogic element in the story is a sign that the author has chosen this means to shape the characters' identities.[8] It guides the audience without allowing them to go off on tangents or lose their ability to focus on the ultimate theme of the story.[9]

Thus, the argument made here is that silence or gaps in speech compose a deliberate narrative strategy. While it does tend to diminish the more typical human dimensions of Abraham's character, it also creates a model of behavior that will become a hallmark for the Israelites in their interactions with YHWH. Furthermore, if these narratives containing a primarily silent Abraham were edited into this form during the post-exilic period, they would be designed to create a clearer understanding of what silent obedience to YHWH means.

Stages of the Story

There are three distinct stages in this silent drama. First is an opening scene with instructions and the silent affirmation of God's command (Gen 22:1–5). Interspersed during the journey is a very brief verbal exchange between Abraham and Isaac over the availability of a sacrificial animal (22:6–8). Finally, the drama ends with a divine intervention, a change in God's command, and a silent return to Beer-sheba following Abraham's successful completion of the test (22:9–19).

The Aqedah does not stand alone without reference to previous narratives in the Abraham cycle. Isaac's position as Abraham's sole heir is tied to the previous expulsion of Hagar and Ishmael (Gen 21:8–21).[10] The link between them is the use of the introductory phrase, "After these things" (22:1a).[11] It functions as a standard time cue and provides a narrative link to the account of Isaac's birth (21:1–7).

Stage One
Making a Silent Journey to Moriah

The Aqedah begins with a prompt for the reader that announces that this story is about how God "tested" Abraham (Gen 22:1b).[12] It is a generic statement that could apply to any test, question, or command.[13] It also establishes from the beginning of the story a particular perspective that gives the narrator's voice complete command of the narrative.[14] The characters will only briefly be allowed to speak. In this way, silence governs their actions, keeps the focus on the terms of the test, and finally affirms Abraham's successful fulfillment of that test (22:15–18).

The story of God's unprompted command that Abraham must take his son Isaac to a designated location and offer him as a burnt offering raises many questions (both ethical and practical) in the mind of the authorial and later audiences.[15] However, only one question is voiced in the narrative, and the answer does not seem very satisfactory given the circumstances. The story has been read differently by the various Abrahamic traditions and the ethical dimensions of the story have been the focus of much of modern Jewish and Christian theological discussion.[16] Ultimately, it is silence—not just mindless obedience to God—that drives the narrative. Silence shapes the story's theological dimensions for the reader.

The action begins when God calls out Abraham by name and our hero simply responds, "Here I am," an acknowledgment of the divine voice and an indication that he is listening.[17] Abraham then stands silent, not making any further statement at this point or asking for further instructions from God. His "attentive silence" reflects respect for a higher power.[18] This is the first of three times in the story that Abraham will answer with this same phrase. It serves as a placeholder without the need for elaboration or further dialogue.

The use of silence as a tool by the author then keeps the reader focused on the progress of the "test." This element takes precedence while continuously building suspense along the way.[19] The author has chosen a narrative technique that sets aside potential storylines or pathways to keep the readers' attention on the goal of determining how and whether Abraham will ultimately pass his test.[20] It is this narrative channeling that establishes barriers to some alternative storylines without irrevocably closing off the possibility of asking questions once the story is completed.

This rhetorical method has been referred to as "deliberate omission" or "suppression" of what others might consider essential to the storyline.[21] Still, it is worth noting that when the ancient authorial audience heard this originally oral composition performed, they possessed cultural conditioning that differs from that of modern readers. Their social background allowed them to perceive silence and its meaning differently from modern readers.[22] As a result, a close reading by modern readers and scholars may result in an uncomfortable feeling of being manipulated by the narrator.

In the Aqedah, God's command that Abraham "take your only son Isaac, who you love" officially excludes Ishmael as Abraham's heir.[23] It also makes it clear that Abraham is to give up without objection the tangible proof of God's fulfillment of the covenant promise of an heir.[24]

That command therefore heightens the tension when Abraham is told to sacrifice his "only son" as a burnt offering.[25]

To a degree this divine command reinforces Sarah's earlier skepticism when the promise of Isaac's birth was spoken (Gen 18:12).[26] It also provides a foundation for the resolution of the story when the angel declares that Abraham has not withheld "your son, your only son" (22:12). However, it sets up a conundrum for Abraham, who sees in this divine command the shattering of his hopes for the future of his household.[27] Recognizing he is at the mercy of a higher power, he accepts this command without question. Abraham silently acts on it despite the fact that his household and the covenant promise are both endangered.[28]

Abraham's silence following YHWH's command has been characterized as a "zero response." There are many other instances in biblical narrative where no response is made to a command, either verbal or nonverbal.[29] Silence in this instance reflects a power relationship that signals the one being commanded accepts that the only response necessary is wordless obedience.[30] Still, given his love for Isaac and Isaac's potential role in the future, it is difficult to accept that Abraham did not cry out, asking God why this sacrifice is necessary.[31] There is no emotional response of love, fear, or hatred of what is being commanded.[32]

The story even lacks any mention of a facial gesture that would indicate Abraham's reaction.[33] Withholding normal human reactions to a crisis serves to demonstrate the degree to which the author continues to control the elements of the story. It highlights the significance of a silent response to the audience. It also sets up the possible conclusion that Abraham has faith in the ultimate outcome of this test. That could explain his willingness to endure the ordeal of taking his son to be sacrificed.

The instruction to Abraham that he is to "go to the land of Moriah ... [and] offer him [Isaac] there as a burnt offering on one of the mountains that I shall show you" could be compared to God's instruction to go "to the land I will show you" (Gen 12:1). In both texts the geographic indicator is nonspecific.[34] Further linking these episodes is the phrase "go forth" (*lek lᵉkā*) that only appears in Genesis 12:1 and in 22:2b. In both cases Abram/Abraham makes no verbal response. He simply "went as the Lord had told him" (Gen 12:4). Such silent obedience is a narrative hallmark of the relationship between Abram/Abraham and YHWH. It stands in stark contrast with Jacob (32:27) and Moses (Exod 3:13), who both ask the deity to reveal his name and purpose.[35]

Abraham's silence may also be based on a cultural acceptance of child sacrifice as an established practice in the ancient Near East.[36] If the authorial audience shares this belief, they will understand why Abraham does not object to YHWH's command. His silence (lack of a response beyond his initial statement of "Here I am") in this case is another form of acknowledgment and an indicator of cultural acceptance of the necessity of the sacrifice.[37] Still, this is likely to be a shock to the later audiences who do not share this cultural worldview. For them this becomes a narrative gap that raises questions about the potential for Abraham's anxiety in the face of this command.[38] It may have also prompted, for both the ancient audience and later interpreters, the question/exclamation of why this outrageous command is necessary given Abraham's certainty that it came from YHWH.[39]

Continuing his silent response, Abraham does not delay in acting on God's command (Gen 22:3a). He rises early, saddles his donkey, orders two servants to accompany them, and takes his son Isaac.[40] The narrative relates these measures without having Abraham speak a word to the servants or his son. There is also no mention of any nonverbal gestures that might ordinarily have accompanied these preparations.[41] Abraham makes no effort here to verbally explain the purpose of the journey or even where they are going. Instead, Abraham's silent preparations keep the focus on forward movement without dialogue or even a leader's instructive monologue.[42]

The author refrains from repeating Abraham's divine instructions for the journey. The audience already knows them. Furthermore, it is important for the universal narrator to be the only "voice" in the story so that the audience's thoughts will not stray or travel along mental tangents. The role of the servants is entirely passive and silent. They are there as "spear-carrier" characters, simply part of the background. In this case, their presence would be an expected element for the audience as a sign of Abraham's status as head of the household and as bodyguards in anticipation of any dangers associated with the journey.

An interesting repetition or demarcation of tasks appears in Genesis 22:3b: cut wood for the burnt offering, set out and travel along the initial route given him by God. In this way the physical travel preparations for the group are separated from the goal of the journey.[43] That in turn serves as a reminder for the audience of what is most important. Abraham continues to demonstrate that he is God's obedient servant, not just a traveler or merchant taking goods to market. There is no other purpose for this journey than to obey God's command to sacrifice Abraham's son.

A time indicator (third day) makes it clear to the audience that they have traveled a fair distance. All human effort during the journey now ceases, and YHWH will direct all further action. But that does not add any greater specificity to which direction they have been traveling, where they are, or the exact location of Moriah. Of course, humans want an immediate response from the deity. More important is creating a mounting sense of tension. That is a common feature of narratives, and three days is the common period in other narratives that is prescribed before God acts or speaks.[44]

The narrative trigger that signals the end of the journey and the next step in the drama occurs when "Abraham looked up and saw the place far away" (Gen 22:4). Abraham understands that he is within reach of his ultimate destination, even though no specific location is provided.[45] There is also encapsulated in this descriptor the sense that they are truly beyond the bounds of settled space in a way that equates with the use of the "wilderness" in other narratives.[46] Abraham's company is now in a silent place where they are more attuned to further instructions from the deity, or, as in this case, to carry out the previous instructions of YHWH.[47]

At this seminal moment, Abraham speaks for the first time during the journey, ordering his "young men" to remain with the donkey while he and "the boy" (no name supplied) go "over there" (unspecified distance) to worship. There is also an assurance that "we will come back to you" (Gen 22:5). That statement, as the audience will discover later in the story, is not entirely true. It may reassure the servants and the boy, but in the end, Abraham will return from Moriah alone.

What is interesting here is that the storyteller finally allows Abraham to break his silence even while he shades the truth by not disclosing more than is necessary. The narrator could have related this information, but it is important for Abraham to make it clear what his purpose is to his servants (worship), and that they are not to accompany him and the boy. It also marks a further leap of faith in which Abraham and Isaac leave the human protection of the servants and the normal world that they represent. Like Moses on Mt. Sinai (Exod 3:2–5) they are about to step into sacred space and into the presence and protection of the deity.

Stage Two
Brief Verbal Exchange between Abraham and Isaac

Without the donkey to help carry the load, Abraham divides the items needed for the sacrifice (Gen 22:6a). Wordlessly, he lays "the wood of the burnt offering" on his son Isaac (a further indicator that the boy is to be a sacrificial victim) and takes the fire and the knife (implements that serve as an indicator that Abraham is the one who will perform the sacrifice). The accompanying phrase (22:6b), "So the two of them walked on together," is the opening of a sandwiching narrative device, an *inclusio*, that will be completed in Genesis 22:8b. It encloses Isaac's question within an otherwise silent journey. Their mutual silence as they travel on to Moriah is a metaphorical expression for their journey that does not require either explanation or questioning. Their emotionless, Zen-like stasis will be broken in the next scene.[48]

The narrative signal that silence is about to end occurs when Isaac, paralleling God's opening statement in Genesis 22:1b, says to Abraham, "Father!" and receives the same response, "Here I am," with the further qualifier "my son." In this way Abraham succinctly acknowledges both his willingness to speak as well as his son's relationship and his right as a member of the household to ask a question (Gen 22:7a). Isaac uses an honorific for Abraham as the father of the household. It also serves as a personal term of endearment reflecting their close relationship, one that is about to be placed in jeopardy between father and son.

Isaac then catalogs what they have brought to this place (fire and wood), and then he asks the all-important question, "Where is the lamb for a burnt offering?" (Gen 22:7b).[49] This query, which at last breaks the silence between them, could have easily been voiced by any reader or member of the audience from the time they began their journey from Beer-sheba. It brings a poignant element into what has been a very wooden narrative with characters acting more like robots than people. In this way the attention of the audience is drawn squarely to the issue of the coming sacrifice. Voiceless from the beginning, Isaac had not questioned the purpose or the timing of the journey when they set out. It may be that he is content with being given the opportunity to accompany his father. Now at the behest of the author, suddenly he wakes up and realizes, as so many of us do when we travel, that we have forgotten something important.

Abraham's almost dismissive response is simply that "God himself will provide the lamb for a burnt offering, my son" (Gen 22:8a).[50] An analysis of this statement, considering the remainder of the narrative, could certainly characterize it as ambiguous and even disingenuous. Even though Abraham is dissembling here, he is telling, even unaware, the truth of what is to come. While it does bring God into the equation as the instigator for their journey and the sacrificial rite, it also discourages any further dialogue.[51] Isaac does not have a rejoinder, since his father's statement has effectively silenced him. He therefore resumes the role of an automaton character. The opportunity for him to display the characteristics of a curious and apprehensive boy has passed. Silence functions as the appropriate punctuation mark for this brief exchange.[52]

Stage Three
Sacrifice Short-Circuited and Test Completed

The narrative uses a series of active verbs to catalog the tasks Abraham must complete to prepare for the sacrifice: he builds an altar, and he lays the wood and the bound (*ʿāqad*) boy on the altar (Gen 22:9). All of this

occurs in silence without any further verbal instructions being supplied
by YHWH or an angel. To be sure, the audience was familiar with
sacrificial rituals and would see these as the appropriate steps. Abraham's
silent activity also follows the pattern of worshipful behavior established
when he silently built altars at Shechem (Gen 12:7), at Bethel (12:8), at
Hebron (13:18), as well as when he plants a tamarisk tree at Beer-sheba
(21:33).[53]

The narrator now certifies that Abraham's company have reached
the place "that God had shown him" (Gen 22:9). Its anomalous
geographic placename of Moriah ties it to the original command (22:2).
The sacred and mysterious character of this place is intentional even
though it will be given a name, *Yahweh-yireh* ("the Lord will provide";
Gen 22:14).[54] It is a place where normal human dialogue is out of place.

As the ritual proceeds, the boy does not cry out. It must now be
apparent to him that he is to be the sacrificial offering. Silence is essential in this case and reflected their presence in sacred space, engaged
in sacred ritual.[55] It adds to the theme of acceptance on the part of the
boy and his father. Furthermore, Abraham, who is about to lose the
son who represents the fulfillment of the covenant promise, does not
raise any objection based on the ethics of human sacrifice or on the
slaughter of an innocent.[56] Unlike many public religious acts, there is
no accompanying prayer, cultic phrase intoned, or invocation of the
deity.[57]

In this instance there is no audience present other than the boy.
Silence as Abraham raises the knife unifies the characters' actions while
allowing for the collective intake of breath by the authorial audience
at this climatic moment.[58] The physical gesture of an upraised hand
signals a clear pause or stillness before the knife is to be ritually plunged
into Isaac's chest (Gen 23:10). Such a silent break might typically signal
either determination or hope for a break in the silence that will resolve
the situation.[59] Here silence must reign supreme as Abraham raises his
hand with the knife to "slaughter" (*šāḥaṭ*) Isaac.[60] The silent ritual of
raising his hand (22:10) is a common gesture used to summon the deity
to participate in the ritual. It gives YHWH the opportunity to choose

whether to accept the sacrifice or to acknowledge that Isaac is the proper choice to live on as Abraham's heir.[61]

The divine response comes as Abraham's muscles tense for the blow. An angel breaks the silence, calling on him to cease and desist (Gen 22:10–12). This is the third time in the narrative that Abraham is addressed by name. Once again, he is allowed to speak and listen as the angel says "Abraham, Abraham?" Reiteration of the name may be for emphasis or to break the spell of obedience to the earlier command.[62] As expected, Abraham once again answers "Here I am" but says nothing more (22:11).

Having passed the test, Abraham is commanded not to harm the boy because he had proven that he "feared" God.[63] He has shown his willingness not to withhold "your son, your only son, from me" (Gen 22:12).[64] The crisis has now passed for the authorial audience and the modern reader. What YHWH had miraculously given to Abraham is now returned to him without the need for a return to the long search for the heir that had culminated in Isaac's birth (21:1–7).[65]

Still, Abraham remains silent despite this last-minute call from the governor commuting Isaac's sentence. He speaks no words of endearment or reassurance to his son, nor does he give thanks to God or show any sign of joy or relief. It is possible that Abraham had mentally transformed Isaac into a nonhuman character that can be sacrificed without passion or restraint. A mental adjustment will be necessary to realign his thinking (Gen 22:10). Silence in this case is more characteristic of Abraham's overall role in the drama. He would have been stepping out of character if he had broken out in a song of thanksgiving. However, the trauma that Isaac endured may also be reflected in his silence. The father-son bond of trust has been broken and will not be restored.[66]

Action resumes when the narrator announces, "Abraham looked up and saw a ram caught in a thicket" (Gen 22:13). The interrupted sacrifice can continue once the struggling animal is disentangled and placed on the altar. As Abraham had said to his son, a proper sacrificial substitute has been provided.[67] Characteristically, Abraham and the ram remain mute during the ceremony that completes the task given to him by YHWH.[68]

Completing their activities at the site of the sacrifice, the place then receives a name to commemorate these momentous events.[69] The act of naming (reported here by the narrator) adds a further layer of sanctity to this location. It adds substance to the later tradition of Moriah as the site of the Temple Mount in the Chronicler (2 Chr 3:1).[70] The reiteration of the covenant promises in Genesis 22:15–18 (compare Gen 15:5) places a narrative period on the scene (i.e., "here ends the lesson"). Note that Abraham, as always, remains silent, neither thanking the deity nor acknowledging the promise given.

One explanation for Abraham's silence in what would ordinarily be an emotion-charged scene may be that he did not believe that YHWH's command would ultimately result in the death of Isaac. It may be that the author has allowed Abraham to mature in his "fear" of YHWH rather than wait on divine intervention.[71] If that is so, then there is no need for Abraham to question YHWH's command and his response to Isaac's question about the sacrificial lamb is not a prevarication designed to settle the boy's concern. It is in fact evidence of Abraham's faith and trust in YHWH to keep the covenant promise even in the face of a difficult command to sacrifice his beloved son.[72] In the end, silence at the time of the command and silence now when the angel releases Abraham from the command shows a mature faith, one that would be an exemplar for the post-exilic audience of this narrative.

All that remains to complete the story is to return home (Gen 22:19). Again, silence reigns as "they arose and went." But Abraham returns alone to his "young men" and Isaac's absence receives no mention. It seems after serving his purpose Isaac is simply written out of the script.[73] This smaller group then "went together" to Beersheba, ironically tying the location of Abraham's household encampment to the place where Hagar and Ishmael received a divine promise of a future after being expelled by Abraham (21:14–20).[74] The use of "together" continues to serve as the terminology for a silent fellowship, but significantly without Isaac in their company. Clearly something has been irrevocably broken between father and son. The relationship and quiet trust expected between Abraham and Isaac cannot and will not be restored. While both Isaac and Ishmael will be present to bury him after Abraham's death, Isaac, Abraham's estranged son, is only said to mourn his mother Sarah after her death (Gen 24:67).[75]

Final Thoughts on Silence and Narrative Gaps

It can be argued that the intentional removal or the suppression of a key character from a narrative is an attempt to silence that character and the perspective that they represent.[76] The traumatic experience at Moriah must have alienated father and son, but Isaac's safe return alone realistically would have necessitated his being old enough to fend for himself during the journey back. More likely, given the use of narrative gaps and silence by the storyteller, Isaac's presence is no longer necessary to this story. Abraham and the narrator have set him aside, leaving him to find his own way home or just be allowed to quietly step off the stage. Whether this would be a problem for the authorial audience is uncertain. Isaac is a subsidiary character in the ancestral narratives, repeating scenes from Abraham's tales (Wife-Sister motif: Genesis 26) and he is quickly shifted aside once Jacob becomes the primary focus of the narratives. If the authorial audience sees Isaac as a less important figure, then his quiet vanishing after the scene at Moriah may not be of particular concern.

Thus, one more gap is not surprising while silence dominates the storyline as it moves toward its end. The narrator supplies no explanation about Isaac's fate after the drama ends on Moriah. He only reemerges after Sarah's death and burial in Genesis 23 when Abraham charges his "oldest" servant to seek out a bride for Isaac in Aramnaharaim and the city of Nahor (Gen 24:1–10). Even then, Isaac has no part in the negotiations, and he is specifically forbidden to accompany the servant (24:6). Only at the end of the narrative does Isaac physically reappear, having settled in the Negeb near Beer-lahai-roi (24:62).[77] He appears silently walking in the field in the cool of the evening, perhaps on a mission to relieve himself. Isaac is then spotted by Rebekah and the servant, and she is subsequently, after Isaac learns of the marriage compact, brought back to "Sarah's tent" as his wife (24:63–67). In this way, Sarah's "voice" (i.e., memory and legacy) is once again heard even in death as Isaac is "comforted" at last by Rebekah's presence as his wife. Fittingly, Isaac remains silent throughout this episode. Rebekah does speak to the servant to verify Isaac's identity (24:65), but the narrator then concludes the story without Isaac speaking a single word to his new bride.

Another group often kept muted or absented in the ancestral narratives is the matriarchs. But the very fact that these women are often marginalized is an indication of the androcentric perspective of the author and the lack of political power by women in that culture.[78] From a strictly rhetorical perspective, there is justification for this narrative technique. It is justified if the intent is to narrow the focus of the story by suppressing a voice that is likely to disagree with the ethics or purpose of the episode. But that raises significant questions about the intent of the storyteller and may be another reflection of a male-dominated society. There would be no compulsion over setting her aside while concentrating on the male characters and their actions.

Perhaps the most glaring absence or suppression in the character list of the Aqedah is Sarah.[79] Some commentators attempt to rearrange the order of the chapters in Genesis to place this story after Genesis 23 and Sarah's death.[80] Midrashic sources (*Genesis Rabbah* 58:5) tie Sarah's death to the grief she experienced upon hearing about the Aqedah or create (*Tanhuma*) an apocryphal dialogue between the ancestral couple in which Abraham provides an excuse for taking Isaac on a journey to educate him about the Creator.[81] Some scholars see Sarah as a "tied" character, with her primary focus on Isaac, and believe she is dependent on his existence to give her status as the mother of the household. This interpretation considers Sarah's absence in Genesis 22 stunning but also suggests that Sarah is the one who should have been tested in this story, not Abraham.[82] Most scholars disagree with this view, noting that it is fundamental that "it is his (Abraham's) test just as it was his call in Gen. 12.1–3, and everything depends upon his trust in the divine promise, not hers."[83]

Rather than relying on these explanations for Sarah's absence, it is just as possible that she does not appear in the Aqedah because it would not be realistic to expect her to remain silent in the face of Abraham's intention to obey God's command to sacrifice their son. Throughout this narrative silence has been the chief feature of the story. The characters, especially Abraham, only speak when called upon and then make only a minimal response. It is more important to the author to keep the focus of the narrative on obedience at the expense of normal dialogue.[84] Sarah would therefore be an intrusive and divisive element if she were part of the scene—one that it would be more difficult to control. She had certainly spoken up in other narratives when she felt her son was in danger. It therefore could be expected that if she was present when Abraham prepared to leave that she would speak up just as boldly as she did when she demanded that her husband expel Hagar and Ishmael from their household (Gen 21:8–13).[85]

As a result, for the Aqedah to have the lasting impact that it did in the Abraham cycle, the author had to submit to a tight staging of events, a reduction in the number of characters, and minimal dialogue. The result is a journey to a mysterious destination with characters who lack normal human emotions. That allows obedience without question to divine command to be upheld as the core value of the story. The only way this can be successfully accomplished is by silencing the characters and sacrificing realism. That restriction is something that the authorial audience may have been able to accept when it is made clear to them that it is a part of building a foundation of faith for their community. Silence in this way is more important than the characters and becomes the primary vehicle for storytelling.

CHAPTER THREE

Silent Characters

BOTH SILENCE AND speech function as standard forms of communication. In daily conversation, when one speaks it is polite to remain silent. Even the pauses in speech provide meaning and assist communication.[1] Within a literary context, silence serves as a major narrative tool for the author of a play or a narrative.[2] When the decision is made to reduce the speech of major characters, that contributes to story development and the amplification of a central theme. Silence can therefore function as a foundational feature within the narrative soundscape, enriching or restricting the characters.[3] When silent auxiliary characters appear in a narrative they often serve as a catalyst for the actions of the major characters. In that way silence can be quite eloquent. For when silent characters react to the words or actions of another character, that elicits a response from the audience or provides a clue to what is happening.[4]

Silent characters are defined here as people who never or infrequently speak during a story. While remaining silent, they play a part and serve as observers of events that can influence an audience's understanding of the scene.[5] Even as voiceless scenery, they obtain credibility and serve the purposes of the author when noticed by the audience. They exist to support characters with speaking parts and, as such, are dispensable. That is why silent characters are often portrayed as two-dimensional.[6]

Being silent does not preclude a character from having an impact on the other characters and the audience. When silent characters are present, the author must find inventive ways to inject their presence into the story without allowing them to become a distraction to the central theme or flow of the story. Once the audience becomes familiar with the cast of characters and their roles, they do not expect verbal responses from silent characters.[7] Silent, auxiliary characters enter as needed and depart the story when their presence is no longer necessary. If they do speak, it is to emphasize a point or to highlight the focus of the narrative.[8]

For example, Sarai is present but never speaks while Abram negotiates their entry into Egypt, even when he allows her to become a part of the pharaoh's harem (Gen 12:10–16). Leah only speaks to name each of her children and, in this way, peoples ten of the tribes of Israel (29:21–30:13). Dinah's rape becomes the basis for the conflict between the city of Shechem and Jacob's sons (Gen 34), but she never speaks during the narrative. The royal court includes female and male servants employed to do a variety of tasks (cook, wet nurse, guard, singer),[9] but they never speak, and their role is simply to people the palace and add a sense of authority to the monarch.

There are also negative examples of silent characters in the text. For instance, women are silently engaged in "weaving for Asherah" (2 Kgs 23:7) and others are quietly "weeping for Tammuz" (Ezek 8:14). Hosea's wife Gomer is part of an extended marriage metaphor portraying the broken relationship between YHWH and Israel. She speaks only two times (Hos 2:5, 7) once to announce her intention "to go after her lovers" (Hos 2:5) and then "to go and return to my first husband" (Hos 2:7).[10] Despite being silenced by Hosea when he casts her out of his house, she is the catalyst for the metaphor and therefore integral to the story. The narrative explores aspects of the honor of the household, the relationship between husband and wife, and the socioreligious constraints placed on them. In the end, what matters for the prophet is the potential for reconciliation (Hos 2:14–20).[11]

If a character remains silent when the audience expects them to speak, then that can draw the audience into the heart of a situation.[12] For example, after Absalom's coup fails and Joab kills him (2 Samuel 18), David sends a pointed message to the priests and elders of the tribes. He asks "why do you say nothing" while others have reaffirmed their allegiance to him as king (2 Sam 19:9–11).[13] Their continued silence could lead to another revolt and David, at this point, needs to solidify his political position. Silence in this instance is a political weapon.

Named but Silent Characters

The case of Rizpah, one of Saul's concubines, provides a prime example of a named but silent character. Her royal connections and tenacity while employing a form of nonverbal communication makes her an intrusive and crucial presence in the narrative. Without speaking a word, her active response to David's actions transcends her silence.[14] Rizpah previously appeared in the text in connection with the feud between Abner and Saul's son Ishbosheth. As a member of the royal harem she had two sons by Saul, and that adds to her potential political worth. The man who claims her after Saul's death could also claim the right to rule.[15] Ishbosheth is justifiably angry believing that Abner has had sexual relations with Rizpah, and he sees this as a gambit toward taking his throne. The dispute then escalates with Abner transferring his political loyalties to David (2 Sam 3:8–12).

That shift in allegiance involves another often-silent female character, Saul's daughter Michal and David's former wife (1 Sam 18:20–23). Saul annuls their marriage and declares David to be an outlaw (19:11–24, 25:44). Now David sees an opportunity to restore a political link to the house of Saul and to strengthen his claim to the throne among the northern tribes.[16] Thus, David demands that Abner restore Michal to him (2 Sam 3:13). For that to happen would require Ishbaal's approval. David's request intimidates Ishbaal (3:14). He immediately orders that Michal be taken from her husband.[17] Abner then brings this female political pawn to David to advance his own political fortunes as well as those of David (3:14–16). Throughout this dramatic power play, Michal remains passive and silent. Neither she nor her husband have any voice or legal options to question David's demand.

Joab's "judicial murder" of Abner ends any possibility of a proposed alliance between Abner and David. Technically, Abner's death is justified as a resolution of a blood feud between their families

(2 Sam 3:23–27), but Joab has been cautioning David about Abner's true motives (3:24–25).[18] It is therefore likely that Abner's assassination was done at the behest of David, despite his public disclaimer and signs of mourning (3:31–29). He simply wished to remove a potentially untrustworthy ally.[19] In quick succession, Ishbaal is assassinated, and his head is brought to David (4:1–7). That leaves David free to step in and accept the invitation to become king of all the Israelite tribes (5:1–3). What had started as a competition over who would claim Rizpah results in a change of dynasties—all sparked by a character who never speaks a word in this drama but serves as the catalyst for the power struggle.

The longer narrative in which Rizpah appears (2 Sam 21) is primarily concerned with Saul as a covenant-breaker. He attempts to wipe out the Gibeonites despite a previous non-aggression agreement that had been made with them (2 Sam 21:2; see Josh 9:15–21; 21:1–2).[20] What results is a divinely-inspired famine, a typical expression of God's displeasure in a land subject to drought and famine.[21] David is then portrayed in a positive light as a diplomat making efforts to uphold the vow made to the Gibeonites, as well as one he made to Jonathan (2 Sam 21:3–9). Revenge for the wrong done to the Gibeonites takes the form of a blood guilt offering of seven of Saul's household. Among those executed are the two sons of Rizpah.[22] David's actions are not simply designed to propitiate the Gibeonites by making a sacrifice that is tied to the barley harvest and intended to propitiate YHWH and end the famine.[23] More importantly for this portion of his political narrative, David demonstrates that he is a worthy successor to Saul. He stands as a ruler who builds up his credit by righting wrongs. More importantly, however, he once again eliminates potential adversaries from among the house of Saul.[24]

Rizpah, caught once again in a political drama, has few options. As a silent character, she decides to employ a nonverbal form of communication.[25] She performs a silent vigil before the bodies of her impaled sons.[26] Her silent pantomime includes a mourning gesture in which she spreads sackcloth over a rock, requiring no words to make it effective (2 Sam 21:10–14).[27] These actions are designed to serve as a counter-narrative to the image of David as a just king. Despite her lack of a speaking part, Rizpah becomes in this brief narrative a central figure, a mother who is now bereft of her children.[28] Her persistence and honorable care for their bodies over the course of an entire season (from the beginning of the barley harvest until the fall rains—mid-April until October) brings attention to David's failure to obey the law. Impaled criminals must not remain unburied overnight (Deut 21:22–23).[29] David remains inactive during this portion of the narrative. He only takes notice of Rizpah's actions when he is told about them (2 Sam 21:11).

Rizpah is both a grieving mother and a political representative of the house of Saul.[30] Her silent vigil publicly shames David and forces him to respond through a similarly public act.[31] David's solution is to take steps that will provide her sons with proper burial while including their remains with the recovered bones of Saul and Jonathan (2 Sam 21:12–14). In this way David appears to enlarge his role as chief officiant for his people, taking the public spotlight away from Rizpah's quiet call for justice.[32]

Another possible interpretation is that the silent figure of Rizpah is responsible for ending the drought rather than David.[33] Still, her actions may have also sealed her fate as a political figure since David does not choose to add her to his household.[34] Rizpah's fate could be compared to that of Saul's daughter Michal, who publicly rebuked David and, although she remained in his household, was intentionally left childless and voiceless (2 Sam 5:16–23).[35]

Another example of mute characters appears in the narrative concerning David's adultery with Bathsheba (2 Sam 11). The author chooses to only allow David a voice here. It is the narrator and the Deuteronomistic editor who shape the narrative in such a way that David's unlawful behavior sets the stage for his confrontation with the prophet Nathan (2 Sam 12).[36] Ultimately, David's own words convict him of an outrageous abuse of power, while the only other person who speaks in the story is Bathsheba's husband Uriah the Hittite.[37]

Bathsheba never speaks in this story. She is a two-dimensional or "flat character" with no narrative depth beyond her beauty and desirability to the king.[38] The only time that she communicates in any form is when she sends a message to David that she is pregnant (2 Sam 11:5). There is also a report of her lamentation after receiving news of her husband's death (11:26). At the end of her period of mourning she immediately marries David and presumably no one counts the months until she gives birth (11:27).

The only other central player in this drama is Bathsheba's husband Uriah the Hittite, one of David's thirty "mighty men" (2 Sam 23:39). Unlike his wife, Uriah is a more developed character, but he only speaks once in the narrative. After receiving news of Bathsheba's pregnancy and realizing he must act quickly before a public scandal erupts, David has Uriah called back from the front where he has been serving as one of Joab's military leaders (11:6). It is David's right as king to order Joab to send Uriah back to Jerusalem. Since there is no reason given for his recall, this could be construed as David exercising his power over Joab. Thus, the general does not ask for an explanation or voice any concern over losing one of his military commanders.

While he is in Jerusalem, there are three encounters between David and Uriah. The first is a perfunctory discussion (not reported in the text) of conditions at the front. David then dismisses Uriah, telling him to return to his house and "wash his feet," a euphemism for having relations with his wife.[39] David does not voice the statement in the form of a command, and therefore Uriah has the right to decide whether to act on David's suggestion.

Uriah instead chooses to sleep in the chamber of the king's guards situated within the entrance of the palace and thereby demonstrates a level of self-control that David clearly lacks.[40] As a result, David becomes increasingly persistent and more pointed in telling Uriah he should go home and have relations with his wife.[41] It is during his second encounter with the king that Uriah at last speaks up. He uses an authoritative tone, invoking the legal stipulation against having relations with his wife while "the servants of my Lord are camping in the open field" (2 Sam 11:11a). Uriah boldly tells his king he "will not do such a thing" and the king has no right to force him to do so (11:11b).[42]

Uriah appears to have made his point by clearly stating that his loyalty to Joab, to his king, and to his men encamped before the enemy prevents him from visiting his wife during his leave (2 Sam 11:11). This argument based on military protocol during a time of war (Deut 23:9–14) exemplifies an accepted tradition of right behavior. Given David's own boast that he has kept his men "clean from women" while they are in the field (1 Sam 21:5), the text indicates a belief that sexual activity is a drain on energy and a source of impurity to be avoided whenever male-exclusive activities are being undertaken. Therefore, Uriah's demure is something that David cannot dispute.[43] In desperation, David arranges for Uriah to become drunk, but Uriah persists in stationing himself in the guardhouse rather than going home to his wife (2 Sam 11:13).[44]

Left with no choice since Bathsheba's pregnancy clock is ticking, David has Uriah carry his own death warrant to Joab. The letter instructs the general to place Uriah in the front lines during the thick of battle and "then draw back" leaving Uriah vulnerable and alone (2 Sam 11:14–15). Joab once again complies, although Uriah's death does not occur in precisely the way that David had commanded (11:17). There would be too many witnesses if Uriah was blatantly left standing by himself on the battlefield.[45] This "cover-up gone wrong" also sets the stage for the confrontation with the prophet Nathan over David's adultery (12:1–14).[46] And it demonstrates that one silent character and one silenced character are at the heart of this narrative.

Adding to this accounting of mute characters in the Davidic cycle of stories, is the brief story of Amasa. Absalom's revolt had sparked another insurrection against David by Sheba and members of the northern tribes (2 Sam 20:1–2). David appoints Amasa as his new military commander (20:4). Amasa previously had commanded Absalom's forces (17:25). This politically based action served as a way of drawing Absalom's followers back to David.[47] It also was a rebuke of Joab for disobeying David's orders to spare Absalom's life (18:5, 12–15). When Amasa, who never speaks a word during this narrative, fails to actively pursue the rebels, Joab takes a hand to deal with the crisis. He visits

Amasa's encampment, greets him affectionately, and then drives a sword into his belly (20:8–10).[48] Amasa's bleeding corpse serves as graphic if mute testimony to the troops that they can no longer delay in the fight against Sheba's followers (20:11–13). The pooling of Amasa's blood speaks louder than words to the previously hesitant troops. Amasa's silence, before and after Joab's visit, then serves to justify a charge that he lacked true loyalty to David.

Nameless, Silent Characters

The author's decision to designate certain characters as silent is often coupled with these characters being nameless. However, nameless people are not always subsidiary characters. Some have a dynamic role to play in the narrative.[49] Nevertheless, many of the nameless in the biblical text are present during crucial scenes but consistently remain silent.[50] They form part of the company of actors in these stories but function more as scenery or as people who are expected or required to be present (i.e., servants or minor characters). Their silence may be based on societal-based disenfranchisement (i.e., women in a patriarchal society) or they are ignored by the other characters in the story.[51] It is the author who chooses not to have them engage in dialogue. Thus, as a narrative tool, both unnamed characters and silence can increase emotion or magnify the level of suspense in a scene.[52]

Nameless, Mute Characters in Legal Situations

Nameless, mute characters commonly appear in biblical law. In fact, the legal statements found in the three collections of law (Covenant Code, Deuteronomic Code, and Holiness Code) are hypothetical situations rather than specific instances involving known persons. As a result, an exchange of dialogue is unnecessary to these descriptive legal statements or during judicial proceedings. Without evidence of their use as legal precedents in actual cases, their purpose seems to be as extensions of the laws in the Decalogue and as a deterrent to inappropriate behavior.[53] For example, in the case of the rebellious son who refuses to obey his father and mother, the parents are required to take him to the city gate to be examined by the elders (Deut 21:18–21). The parents, serving as the legally requisite two witnesses, speak only a formulaic accusation against him, charging him with disobedience, gluttony, and drunkenness.[54] The elders do not give the son the opportunity to make any rebuttal testimony, and then "all the men of the town" stone him to death.[55] As is the case in many of the legal scenarios, this one is governed in its entirety by ritual performance and staged pronouncements. It serves as a corollary to the commandment to "honor your father and your mother" (Exod 20:12).

Nevertheless, several legal situations described in the biblical text are relevant to the discussion of silence. Those accused of a crime seldom speak on their own behalf. For instance, the young woman accused by her husband of not being a virgin at the time that their marriage was consummated stands mute. Her father must then act to uphold the honor of his household. He presents to the elders at the city gate the physical evidence of her virginity on the wedding night and voices a ritualistic oath of clearance (Deut 22:13–22).[56]

Even when a woman must undergo a test or an ordeal to prove guilt or innocence, the ritual only allows the accused to take an oath and await the outcome of the test that will determine her fate. That is the basis for the *Sotah* ritual (Num 5:11–31). The legal situation portrayed here centers on the activities of three hypothetical, unnamed characters: a husband, his wife, and a priest. As a legal scenario, it strictly follows a pattern of ritual pronouncements and affirmations rather than dialogue. Lacking witnesses, the case cannot be resolved using normal legal processes.[57] Therefore, the jealous husband must resort to an elaborate ceremony conducted by a priest. In this way he can satisfy his concerns over whether his wife has been unfaithful. He is to take her and present a "grain offering of jealousy, a grain offering of remembrance" to the priest (5:14–15).[58] The offering serves as a vehicle to "recall" the alleged wrongdoing and in this way bring to light what will result in the inevitable punishment for this indiscretion.[59]

What follows is an orchestrated ritual in which the priest concocts a potion comprised of dirt from the floor of the tabernacle, holy water, and the dissolved ink from a written list of curses, creating the "water of bitterness."[60] The assumption here is that the wife freely submits to this test as she is set "before the Lord" for judgment. Her hair is disheveled, and she must hold in her hand the typical portion of the grain offering. At that point, the priest requires her to take the oath that places a curse on her head based on her actions (Num 5:19–20). He then speaks the curse of execration calling on YHWH to determine her guilt. Evidence of her guilt occurs after drinking the potion when she suffers a prolapsed uterus and resultant sterility (5:21–22a). In that way, rather than having the woman speak during the ritual, it is her body that speaks to her innocence or her guilt.[61]

Both statements by the priest are quotations from the ritual text rather than his own words.[62] The only words spoken by the unnamed woman during this intimidating performance are "amen, amen" (Num 5:22). These words also would be a part of the ritual and they simply function as her affirmation as a participant. If the ordeal or test demonstrates her innocence, the woman will subsequently be able to conceive.[63] She will then have freed her husband from his "spirit of jealousy" (5:29–31). Despite her stolid and obedient behavior, it will not free her from the public humiliation associated with enduring the ritual or from the voices of her neighbors.

Nameless, Mute Characters in Narrative

Among the nameless, silent characters that appear in biblical narrative are Lot's wife and his daughters in Genesis 19:1–29. During the scene in which the men of Sodom demand that Lot must send out his visitors (Gen 19:4–5), Lot instead offers to give his two virgin daughters to the crowd "to do to them as you please" (19:7–8). At no point do the unnamed daughters object, remaining silent and passive as they await the outcome of Lot's offer. Of course, as the head of household Lot has the right to speak for his family, and his hospitality obligations to his guests guide his statement to the assembled crowd.[64] If this experience traumatizes the daughters, that could explain why they seek revenge on their father in the subsequent episode.[65] Lot's unnamed wife's only role in the story seems to be to demonstrate the consequences of disobedience. She looks back at Sodom and is turned into a pillar of salt (Gen 19:26). She never raises any objections to Lot's offer of their daughters to the crowd or to their escape from the city.

Interestingly, it is Lot who is mute while his daughters speak up in the attached etiological story about the origin of Moab and Ammon (19:30–38). Finding themselves housed in a cave after the destruction of Sodom and Lot's failure to stay in the village of Zoar (19:30), they realize that they have no hope of an arranged marriage with their household being complicit in Sodom's destruction. Therefore, like Judah's daughter-in-law Tamar (Gen 38:11–26), who also had been relegated to a childless and husbandless state, the daughters plan together to get Lot drunk and on successive nights have sexual relations with him.[66] By means of this trickery, both become pregnant, and their sons become the founders of Israel's Transjordanian neighbor states. The incestuous origins of Moab and Ammon stand as a political polemic against them, suggesting that this episode may be an addendum to the larger narrative.[67]

What is interesting in this examination of silent characters is that Lot remains mute throughout this last section of the narrative. Lot neither instructs his daughters about their living arrangements nor condemns them for their incestuous rape while he was drunk. It would have been his responsibility to arrange marriages for them, but instead he is cowering in fear in this isolated cave.

Lot's passive behavior has led some commentators to suggest that this is an example of an inverted or "world turned upside down" story in which Lot ceases to exercise his responsibility as head of household and receives his just rewards for his earlier callous behavior toward his daughters.[68] His behavior after the destruction of Sodom, the loss of his wife, and his ignominious flight from Zoar may show the degree to which his decisions cost him and explain why he then becomes a mute character. In fact, like his daughters, Lot is a victim of traumatic circumstances, and he has been stripped of his authority, silenced, and left a pitiful shell of a character.[69] It also closes the door quite firmly on any possibility that he will become the heir to Abraham's covenantal promise.

Judges 19 contains a parallel story to that of Lot in Sodom (Gen 19:1–14). It follows the same storyline but with a twist that creates a polemic against Gibeah, the Tribe of Benjamin, and King Saul.[70] The story depicts the same situation in which a guest is endangered by a demanding crowd of men outside the host's door (Judg 19:22–25). The variation in the storyline occurs when their host unceremoniously throws the visiting Levite's unnamed concubine out to the mob (19:25). These brutal men ravage her while her husband and their host resume their dinner. It is this abused Levite's concubine, like the unnamed daughters of Lot, who serves as an example of a subsidiary or secondary character who remains silent throughout her ordeal.

In the Judges 19 version, only male voices are heard, but they, like the concubine, are all unnamed and therefore judged to be worthless "nobodies."[71] The victimized and nameless concubine's only example of communication is in her final gesture of falling prostrate at the door of the Ephraimite's house with her hands extended across the threshold (Judg 19:26–27). Since liminal space like a city gate or the entrance way or threshold of a house are among the places of judgment within Israelite law, her mute but understandable judicial gesture indicts those within the house who sacrificed her life for theirs.[72]

Even this eloquent gesture provides her with no respect. The Levite unceremoniously commands her to get up so they can depart (Judg 19:28). Her lack of response adds to the irony of his unfeeling behavior and adds to her silent, posthumous formal accusation.[73] With no other recourse, he packs her body on his donkey, dismembers her corpse and uses the pieces to provide a silent testament to the criminal act committed at Gibeah. Using her as silent evidence of an atrocity, he harangues the tribal leaders to spark a civil war among the Israelite tribes and to punish the Benjaminites (19:27–30). Amid the cry for battle lies the unnamed, dismembered, and silent concubine. She has no voice to refute the Levite's inflammatory and false statements.

An extended story recording the feud between Jeroboam I and the prophet Ahijah provides another excellent opportunity to explore the use of an unnamed, silent character in biblical narrative.[74] In this case, it is Jeroboam's wife who takes a leading role while never speaking a word. Her silence throughout the story reinforces her helpless situation. She serves as the pawn of first her husband and then the prophet. They order her about but give her no voice in crucial portions of the narrative.

The story begins when the prophet Ahijah, using a garment motif gesture, tears up a new robe and gives Jeroboam ten of the twelve pieces indicating that God has chosen him to rule the ten northern tribes after the death of Solomon. There is no anointing ceremony at this point in 1 Kings 11:26–40, only a reiteration of the covenant promise and a "directive speech" obligating Jeroboam to keep God's statutes and ordinances (1 Kgs 11:37–38).[75] Like David, the prophet promises him (2 Sam 7:11–12), "an enduring house" if he listens to, walks in the way, and keeps God's statutes. There is no mention in the text of Jeroboam responding in any way to the prophet's actions or words. The audience may well have recognized this non-response as a form of nonverbal acquiescence, a "zero response."[76] Note in confirmation that neither Saul (1 Sam 10:1–8) nor David (1 Sam 16:13) nor Solomon (1 Kgs 1:39) voices his acceptance when he is anointed king. For Solomon, the ritual act of his anointing by Zadok is enough to elicit a response from the people acclaiming his right to be king (1:40).

Ahijah's commissioning had given Jeroboam the divine right to rule the northern tribes of Israel (1 Kgs 11:26–38). Jeroboam, however, fails to uphold the terms set forth by God to "walk in my ways" (11:38). In fact, his response, once he became king of the northern tribes, is not a verbal one. Instead, he establishes cult centers at Bethel and Dan as part of a political program designed to control cultic practices and places and demote the importance of Jerusalem's temple. His actions are an example of "self-will and self-deception" that the Deuteronomist labels as Jeroboam's sin. They are painted as the cause of political instability and internecine strife that eventually results in the fall of the northern kingdom.[77] That becomes clear when Jeroboam attempts to dedicate the shrine at Bethel. The public ceremony is disrupted by "a man of God from Judah." The king stretches out his arm in a threatening gesture, and then is forced to humble himself and ask for a healing prayer from his unnamed, prophetic critic when his arm is withered (13:1–10).

It is at this point in the narrative that the original promise of "an enduring house" returns to center stage. The operative phrase is "at that time." It forms an inclusio with Jeroboam's first encounter with Ahijah that is also heralded with the phrase "about that time" (1 Kgs 11:29).[78] Events then progress with the introduction of two silent characters, Jeroboam's son and presumed heir, Abijah, and his mother.[79] The son has become ill and, facing this threat to the continuation of his family's rule of Israel, Jeroboam chooses to send his unnamed wife to consult the now-blind prophet.[80] His decision to send her, rather than approach the prophet himself, might be attributed to his bad experience with the unnamed prophet highlighted in 1 Kings 13, but it could also be a political snub, with the king sending a lesser representative rather than going himself.[81] Jeroboam's use of an imperative verb (Go!) suggests the "intensity, rapidity, and purposefulness" of her task, but it may also be an indication of her inferior status as a woman and not a working member of his court.[82]

The question arises whether the author deliberately silenced and removed the psychological responses of Jeroboam's wife for the purposes of this story.[83] Perhaps the woman is cowed by her husband's command or is simply willing to do anything to help her child.[84] Wordlessly, she carries out his command and, as we will see, she remains a silent character throughout the story despite its emotional overtones.[85]

Jeroboam orders his wife to disguise herself in preparation for visiting the prophet (1 Kgs 14:2). Since Ahijah is blind, it seems unlikely that her disguise is an effort to fool him in this way. Instead, and more likely, Jeroboam is sensitive about having any of his political allies or enemies see his wife, a royal representative of his court, consulting a prophet. Jeroboam had previously separated himself from association with religious figures that he could not control.[86]

Ahijah, despite his blindness, immediately identifies her as the wife of Jeroboam and questions her attempt to disguise herself (1 Kgs 14:6). He then turns the tables and never gives her the opportunity to speak. Even though Jeroboam had sent the queen to consult him, Ahijah now stands forth as the one who has come to her to pronounce in a fierce torrent of words God's judgment on the house of Jeroboam. In that way, he parallels the original scene in which Jeroboam had sent her on this mission. Instead of Jeroboam giving her a command and a task to perform, now it is God through the prophet telling her to "go to Jeroboam" (14:7).[87] Although she may have been startled into silence by the harshness of the prophecy, it is characteristic of the narrator to keep her silent. She expresses no hesitation or gesture of grief at the approaching death of her son.[88] Putting a period on this narrative, she simply returns to Tirzah (14:17) where, as predicted, the son dies.[89] Silent to the end, there is no reaction provided in the text about her loss.

It is this unnatural lack of response that prevents the audience from empathizing with this woman and her child. Ordinarily, the audience would expect that this woman would make an unconscious physical reaction (gestures, facial expressions, or body posture) in the face of such tragic news and events, but the text reveals nothing about the strain placed upon her.[90] The narrator does leave a few obvious questions about this anonymous woman's lack of response unanswered. It is likely that her voice has become victim to the author's desire to focus exclusively on the sins of Jeroboam.[91] That authorial decision parallels the exclusion of Sarah from the Aqedah (Gen 22), preventing her from expressing opposition to the sacrifice of her son Isaac. It seems that Jeroboam's desire to control the actions of others is based on his fear of the prophet. In any case, his actions backfire when he tries to "hoodwink" God and the prophet.[92]

Concluding Thoughts

Written narrative and legal statements or case studies provide a fertile opportunity for an author to utilize silent characters. They augment the story by their silent presence without getting in the way of the theme or focus. Major characters can therefore use these intentionally silent actors as the foil or simply as part of the background, like a spatial or geographical setting. They can help move a scene along, serve as examples, or just represent expected "decoration." Thus, a king must have his court with guards, advisers, and supplicants. But none may speak unless given leave to do so.[93] Similarly, when crafting a legal scenario, it is more important to lay out the basics of the case, describe the rituals involved, and detail the aspects of reward and punishment than to include dialogue. And, in the shaping of a narrative, it is best to recognize what is most important to reveal to the audience. Scenery may evoke a response, but when a character speaks it draws attention back to the plot. Silence and silent characters derive their significance by "being there" as much as by any words they might speak.

CHAPTER FOUR

Silence and Silencing

WHEN SPEAKING WE typically use silence to provide emphasis or clarity to our words. Silence, when used efficiently, can be as eloquent and refreshing as any spoken phrase.[1] It can express a collective opinion about a speaker's words or indicate an unwillingness to participate. Without silence there is nothing but continuous sound running on forever that garbles or covers up meaning. Silence therefore can be restorative, allowing a person to be introspective without interruption and appreciate the natural world or simply a place where we feel comfortable and safe.[2]

Silences for whatever reason have significance. Deep silence between intimates serves as an expression of shared experience, trust, love, and sometimes hate.[3] Even the pause between the blasts of a trumpet have meaning if only to allow them to clearly articulate each note and thus provide the correct signal for action on a battlefield or to initiate movement.[4] For example, the Israelite households could be distinguished during the Passover event by the silence of the dogs who neither barked nor growled at the Israelites (Exod 11:7). At the same time the Egyptian households were in an uproar over the death of their firstborn. In this way, silence serves as a demarcation between sounds and a means of separating these two groups.

Silencing is an active imposition of silence.[5] Silencing can be both a physical reaction and a cultural phenomenon. Cultural differences also play a part. For instance, some cultures express anger through their silence rather than by engaging in outraged speech. Others allow silence to serve as an expression of respect, surprise, joy, uncertainty, sorrow, or fear.[6] Silencing may occur when a quiet moment is needed to contemplate one's next word or action.[7] Silencing occurs when something shocking happens that leaves people speechless with perplexity or shock.[8] Silencing occurs when honor or respect for someone results in refraining from meaningless speech or commotion. Silencing occurs when a powerful person or group demands that others remain or become silent. It is emotion-ladened, psychologically driven, and can serve as a vehicle of oppression. Silencing also occurs at death when a person breathes their last and their voice is forever stilled (Gen 25:17; 35:29).

Silencing as a Physical Reaction

Silencing is a reaction to a variety of bodily responses that include being overwhelmed by severe physical or mental fatigue. That is the case with Daniel who is reduced to speechlessness after fasting for three weeks and receiving a vision of the conflict between the Prince of Persia and the angel Michael (Dan 10:15–19).[9] Another common experience that may trigger silence is a social mistake such as a breach of manners or an unexpected event. A person or a group of people may be so taken aback that they are speechless when something happens that seems out of character with established practice. That is the case with Joseph's brothers when he gives Benjamin a five-fold portion at dinner (Gen 43:33).[10] Similarly, when Joseph questions his brothers about their father, they are so terrified that they are unable to respond (45:3). The brothers are not exhibiting hostility or uncooperativeness, but they are just overwhelmed by their powerless state and the setting in the Egyptian court. Startlement also seems to be the basis for the reaction of kings to the exaltation of Second Isaiah's "Suffering Servant" (Isa 52:13–15). His unexpected transformation of fortunes from an object of ridicule into someone to whom homage is to be given requires the kings to reevaluate the power of his God.[11]

Shock is an experience that can be used to silence someone.[12] Aaron is struck dumb after his sons are killed by YHWH for offering "unholy" fire.[13] His speechlessness is a result of his acceptance of divine judgment and personal bewilderedness. Therefore, he finds himself in no position to refute Moses's rebuke about inappropriate ritual offerings or to question the command not to mourn for his sons (Lev 10:1–5).[14] Shock over their immense loss may also be the cause for the "elders of the daughter of Zion" to sit on the ground in silence (Lam 2:10). With its palaces and temple in ruins, the personified city of Jerusalem and its former leaders can only bow their heads and accept the derision of their enemies (Lam 3:16). They are reduced to sitting alone in the silence imposed on them by YHWH (3:28).[15] It is the "separation from YHWH's protective presence" that has shocked them into silence as they react to the feeling of abandonment.[16]

That is certainly the case with the silence that occurs in Jerusalem after the public execution of the unpopular and murderess Queen Athaliah (2 Kgs 11:1–20).[17] A tremendous turmoil had shaken the city with the tearing down of the temple of Ba'al and the blaring trumpets that had signaled the political change of regime (11:13–18). There was then a collective sigh of relief expressed by the quieting of the city and its people following this frenzy of sounds (11:20).[18] The period of "quiet" serves as the sign of lessening tensions and general relief at the end of an unpopular reign.[19]

A sense of futility such as that felt by Job's three "friends" can lead to frustrated silence. In their case, they realize that they are having no effect on a character who is "righteous in his own eyes" (Job 32:1) and they "become dismayed." As a result, they cease to offer any further arguments and stand silent (32:15).[20] In another instance, Naomi provides her two daughters-in-law with a list of arguments for why they should return to Moab. Her rhetoric is quite emphatic and emotional, calling on them to seek a better, more fulfilling life in their own country. However, she abruptly refrains from urging Ruth to return to Moab when this very assertive younger woman pledges not to abandon her mother-in-law (Ruth 1:18).[21] It is simply that no further argument is likely to make any difference, and resigned silence is better than wasted words.

Sorrow can result in silencing the voices of those who mourn just as joy causes people to raise their voices in song and celebration.[22]

Mourning can be the reaction of an individual to personal bereavement or a collective, petitionary response by the people to a national disaster.[23] Within the range of mourning practices, some may be uncontrollable and thus psychological or emotion-based.[24] Showing emotion without speaking, David puts on sackcloth, fasts, and lays on the ground before the bed of his dying child in a petitionary form of mourning. His quiet stance only ends when David is told by his advisers that the child has died—and at that point, he resumes his normal duties (2 Sam 12:16–19).[25]

When YHWH tells Ezekiel that his wife is about to die, the prophet is commanded not to engage in the normal emotional display of weeping (Ezek 24:15–18). While his personal loss is symbolic of the loss to be suffered by the exiles as they are taken from a destroyed Jerusalem, both he and they are startled into an abnormal response.[26] Rather than voice their normal outward expressions of grief, they are reduced to a sort of involuntary moan or murmur that escapes them like a sigh.[27] While they may be steeped in grief, the shunning of mourning activities and their silence represents an acceptance of the fall of Jerusalem and a submergence of acceptable emotions.[28]

The prophets use the transition from exultant behavior to mourning and an end to the sounds of joy as part of their warning to the nation that God's impending judgment is at hand (Isa 3:18–26; 24:7–8).[29] That sullen silence is then reversed, with joy and expectation returning for the people in the prophets' restoration oracles, such as Jeremiah's Book of Consolation (Jeremiah 30–31).[30] In a similar way, the author of Psalm 30:12 speaks of the transformation of those who mourn silently into those whose joy breaks out in dance and songs of thanksgiving.

In their oracles against the nations, the prophets often depict the people who have served as Israel's enemies mourning over their reduced state.[31] For instance, Jeremiah describes how the Philistine cities of Gaza and Ashkelon are in mourning after being devastated by the pharaoh's armies. They shave their heads and gash their flesh and are then silenced in their despair (Jer 47:5).[32] Their silencing reflects YHWH's authority and explains their inability to perform overriding standard practices such as assisting children during the disaster (47:3).[33] The mourners' silence stands in contrast to YHWH's insatiable sword that cannot be sheathed or stilled (47:6–7).[34]

In another instance, Second Isaiah triumphantly prophesies YHWH's humiliation of the "virgin daughter of Babylon." She is now forced to grovel in the dust in her grief rather than sit on her throne. Stripped of her finery and required to sit in silence like a slave, she no longer bears her royal titles as "the mistress of kingdoms" (Isa 47:1–5). Silence in this case is the result of "defeat, suffering, or oppression" and it contrasts with the former state of Babylon as the one who could command other nations.[35]

Silencing in Legal Situations

Silencing functions in a variety of settings including within a legal framework. The Holiness Code lists moral actions designed to create a holy nation. For instance, the Israelites are forbidden to "revile the deaf" (Lev 19:14). Those with a physical disability are protected from being silenced based on their inability to hear or speak effectively. Specifically, no one is to swear an oath before a deaf person since they would be unable to hear or respond to defend themself.[36] Another legal statement contains the multifaceted law related to female vows (Num 30). The legal status of the woman (unmarried, married, widow, or divorced) is the basis for each of these segments. Thus, when an unmarried woman voices a vow or a pledge of a votive offering and her father chooses to stand mute (literally, "makes himself deaf to her") that is taken as implicit agreement on his part for her to do so.[37] It is only if he raises an objection that her vow is abrogated, and God forgives her for not fulfilling the vow and making the offering (Num 30:3–5).[38] The same holds true for the vow taken by a married woman and is dependent on whether her husband speaks no objection (30:6–8).[39] For our purposes, the significance is legally bound up in male silence.

In a judicial context, silencing is the ultimate result of the imposition of capital punishment. The "stubborn and rebellious son" is charged with neither listening to his parents nor obeying them after numerous admonishments. They take him to the city gate, and they provide detailed accusations before the elders (Deut 21:18–21). Left to his own devices, the son could not only disrupt the normative expectations between parents and child, but he could then progress to endangering his family's household resources through his gluttony and drunkenness (21:20). All these activities set a bad example for others to follow. With the potential apparent to create a social evil, it becomes clear that it and he must be purged from their community in a way that is final: the silence of death.[40]

The sentence of capital punishment also appears in narratives that contain legal connotations. For example, Jezebel utilizes two false witnesses to arrange the "judicial murder" of Naboth (1 Kgs 21:8–14) and his sons (2 Kgs 9:21).[41] After Naboth is accused of cursing God and the king, he is taken outside the city and stoned. Ordinarily, this form of silencing would also remove Naboth's household's name from the Israelite community, in much the same way as Achan's when he and his family were stoned for violating the *herem* at Jericho (Josh 7:25–26).[42] However, because his fate is referenced several times, it could be said that his voice was silenced but his name continued to live in memory.

Silencing as a Reflection of Power and Authority

Silencing is often employed as a dynamic tool designed to demonstrate the power and authority of forces that cannot be resisted without harsh consequences. Sometimes this is a punitive measure and sometimes a reaction to the exercise of power. That comes clear in the "Song of Moses" when the chiefs of Edom and Moab are so dismayed at the power displayed by YHWH on behalf of the Israelites that they are reduced to stillness "like a stone" (Exod 15:15–16). The decision to remain or stand silent can thus be based on resignation to one's fate in the face of overwhelming power. During Joshua's battle with the coalition of five kings, the slaughter is so overwhelming that "no one dared to speak against any of the Israelites" (Josh 10:20–21).[43] Their mass silence is equated with surrender just as Joshua's humiliation (10:22–24) and execution of the kings effectively silences the voices of the leaders of the enemy (10:26–27).

One sign of authority is the ability to command silence. When the command to be silent is obeyed and is accompanied by attentive silence, then the one in authority gains more legitimacy.[44] In Zechariah's prophetic vision, YHWH is accorded due respect and reverence when "all flesh" is called on to be silent. That in turn becomes a keystone of a deity when roused "out of his holy habitation" to begin the work of restoration of the exiles (Zech 2:11–13).[45] Commanded silence also serves as a warning to those proud officials in Judah who have engaged in idolatry and turned their backs on YHWH that the "Day of the Lord" and their judgment is at hand (Zeph 1:4–7).[46] The command to be silent then becomes an unequivocal instruction to listen in the face of YHWH's manifested power and the mounting disaster faced by a disobedient people (Amos 8:3).[47]

Muzzled speech or commanded silence appears in the encounter between the scouts of the migrating tribe of Dan and the Levite, who had been serving as household priest for Micah in the hill country of Ephraim (Judg 17–18). There is only minimal dialogue between Micah and the Levite. His role is to simply officiate over the ritual conducted in the house shrine along with its teraphim, ephod, and idol. When the Danite scouts stop at Micah's house, they ask the Levite to "inquire of God" about the success of their mission, and they receive an ambiguous response that they "are under the eye of the Lord." Later the larger company of Danite warriors come and loot Micah's shrine. They take his sacred objects and provide the Levite with a job offer to serve a tribe rather than a single individual, and he accepts. The critical point where silence comes into this narrative is when the Danites command the Levite to "keep quiet" while they plunder the house shrine.[48] "Silenced speech" in this case is reinforced with a humiliating gesture, to "put his hand over his mouth" (Judg 18:19).[49]

Silencing can suppress the views of those who disagree with the official opinion expressed by the majority.[50] The practice of silencing can result from a belief that these minority views are dangerous to society or undermine the political position of the government.[51] That belief can therefore justify acts of violence to silence the offending voice, such as the threat made by the people of Anathoth to kill Jeremiah if he continues to prophesy in the name of YHWH (Jer 11:21–23).[52] There are several other occasions when Jeremiah's foes plot to prevent him from speaking his message, and these include beatings (20:2), imprisonment (32:3), and threats of violence (15:10; 17:15).[53] In addition to bringing false charges against the prophet, they even espouse cutting out his tongue to effectively silence his divine compulsion to speak (18:18).[54]

Censure or suppression of ideas or opinions may for a time satisfy the desire of the majority voice to silence voices or ideas that it considers dangerous or counterintuitive.[55] When Jeremiah is arrested and placed in confinement (Jer 37:11–16), it is both the message of the prophet and the word of YHWH that the king's advisers wish to suppress.[56] King Jehoiakim's act of bravado in burning Jeremiah's scroll (36:23) punctuates his efforts to control the message, and the lack of any stark reaction by his advisers (36:24–26) is an indication that he has at least temporarily achieved his goal.[57] Ultimately, he is left with ashes and the position of being a puppet ruler while the Babylonians and Egyptians compete for his territory, and Jeremiah proceeds to dictate another scroll (36:32).

Submitting to silencing may occur when someone is afraid of social isolation, amazed, or wishes to avoid being out of touch with common beliefs or ideas.[58] That may be the case when Hananiah publicly confronts Jeremiah. Both men have previously been recognized as a YHWH prophet. Hananiah's prophecy that YHWH would "break the yoke of Babylon" requires Jeremiah to deal with a statement that contradicts his own call for submission to the yoke of Babylon. It also offers the much more popular theme of peace and restoration of the sacred vessels from the temple (Jer 28:2–4). Jeremiah responds with a sarcastic "Amen!" but then challenges his prophetic rival citing Deuteronomy (Deut 18:22). He says when prophets prophesy peace they are certified as true prophets "when the word came about" (Jer 28:8–9).[59]

At that point, Hananiah must respond with a physically startling gesture. He punctuates his opposition by violently breaking off the ox yoke that Jeremiah has been wearing to physically symbolize his prophecy (Jer 28:10–11a). Jeremiah is initially nonplussed by Hananiah's strategy of intimidation. He exits the public scene and he remains silent for a time (28:11b).[60] Ultimately, if silencing such as this is successful, then the range of opinion is narrowed until only one viewpoint is acceptable and approved by a community.[61] However, Jeremiah does return to the fray with a new prophecy of an "iron yoke" being placed on the nations who oppose Babylon. Jerusalem's direr fate is coupled with the prediction of Hananiah's death within a year (28:14–16). In that way, both a false prophet and his false prophecy is silenced.

Silencing by Those in Authority

Authority and power complement each other. However, it is authority that makes it possible for power to be exercised.[62] Power is ability and authority is the permission needed to use power. Both power and authority can be gauged by the extent to which an individual or a group is able to influence or control other individuals or groups.[63] Authority obtains its inherent abilities through interpersonal association.[64] Its willingness to be employed is based on a variety of motivations and situations. For instance, the ability to command silence reflects the power of an individual or group either to lead or to intimidate others. That command to be silent can include not allowing the voices of people who have no power or significance within society to be heard.[65] They can be silenced by force, but it is just as effective to minimize their contributions to the point where others pay no attention to them. In the process, they become invisible and silent.[66]

A sign of personal authority and an indication of the level of respect or fear held by a leader is therefore signified by exercising their ability to silence and control others.[67] It is within the silence of the subordinate that the one in authority is assured of either consent or surrender.[68] An example is when Nehemiah confronts the nobles and officials in

Jerusalem over their practice of charging interest on loans that had led to the poor being forced into debt slavery (Neh 5:1–13). The reaction of these wealthy leaders of the community was to simply stand silent, incapable of mounting a defense of their oppressive practices in the face of a stronger authority (5:8).[69]

Another demonstration of that power is in Elijah's repeated command that the unnamed "company of prophets" be silent when they speak about his being taken away by YHWH (2 Kgs 2:3–5).[70] Their silence then becomes a sign of their respect and trust in the prophet.[71] The audience is forced to wait until the critical moment when Elijah "ascends in a whirlwind into heaven" and in the process the author builds suspense at each reiteration of this silencing command (2:11).[72]

Respect of those in authority is often the basis for obedience. When the actions of a community's or nation's leaders damage that respect, then it can be expected that their authority will begin to crumble. Thus, when Saul becomes angry over David's growing popularity after his success as a military commander (1 Sam 18:6–8),[73] he reacts violently without thinking. At one point just the sight of David causes Saul to throw a spear at him while he was playing a lyre in the palace (18:10–11). As Saul's hostility grows, David then escapes the palace and Saul's rage. That in turn leads to David making a pact with Jonathan that will eventually increase Saul's ire. During the fast-approaching New Moon festival, David would be expected to sit at table with the king (20:1–6). Jonathan assures David of his support but acknowledges that David's absence at this crucial time would be noticed. The king will interpret David's lack of physical presence and his missing voice as a sign of insurrection and will increase his hatred of David (20:30–34). Silencing in this case is a result of Saul's unhinged behavior rather than his authority.

Authority also becomes questionable when there is no response from subordinates to the command to speak or act. King Saul discovers this problem during his war with the Philistines. Desperate for a victory, Saul "laid an oath" on his troops prior to the battle that they must fast until they have defeated the enemy (1 Sam 14:24). The received biblical text declares this to be a "rash act" and then enumerates the basis for the eventual conflict between the king and his military commanders.[74] First, the king's son Jonathan unwittingly violates the oath and eats some honey (14:27), and then the famished troops eat meat without draining the blood first (14:34; see Lev 17:10-14). When YHWH refuses to answer Saul's query about further military actions, the king resorts to casting lots to determine the sin that was blocking divine assistance (14:37-38).[75] When the lot falls to Jonathan, the king proposes to execute his son, but his commanders stand silent refusing to turn him over for execution. In this case, their refusal to answer matches YHWH's refusal to respond. Further casting of the lots confirms that it is Saul who is in the wrong and his authority is significantly damaged (14:41-45).[76]

Commanded silence can cool down a potential confrontation or restrain heightened emotions.[77] Samuel calls on an agitated King Saul to stop making excuses for his failure to complete the ḥerem against the Amalekites. The prophet tells him he must listen instead to the words of YHWH rather than continue to justify himself (1 Sam 15:16). Cowed into silence by this command, Saul resignedly says "speak." High emotions are also evident in the story of Ezra's covenant renewal ceremony (Neh 8:1-12). After Ezra reads the law, the people weep (8:10). The Levites then proclaim that "this day is holy to the Lord" and not a time for mourning or weeping. In this way, they "still" the people's sorrow and give them license to celebrate in a new understanding of the law (8:11-12).[78]

Unfortunately, a command to become silent does not always work. Caleb makes the valiant effort to quiet the people and their growing apprehension after they hear the discouraging report of the spies who were sent by Moses into Canaan (Num 13:30).[79] However, his rallying call is ignored, and instead of following him to conquer the land, they cry out in despair (14:1).[80] On the other hand, when a leader commands silence and gets it from the "audience" (followers, guards, advisers) that leader is gratified to receive the desired expression of obedience.[81] That is the case when Eglon the Moabite king calls for "silence" after being told by Ehud that he has a "secret message" for the king's ears alone. The king's call for "silence" immediately results in a clearing of the room so that only he can hear this divine word (Judg 3:19).[82]

For demagogues who have not yet achieved the power they crave, haranguing a crowd using emotion and reason, resulting in raising the people's temper to commit acts of violence or insurrection, is more typical. In feeding on the sense of injustice and foreboding for the future, their goal is to get the audience to cry out their allegiance and acceptance of the demands of the speaker.[83] For them, enforced silence only becomes a goal once they are in power and are controlling the official message. Then silencing becomes an exemplification of their authority.

We see this in action when Absalom "stole the hearts of the people" with his rhetoric and promise of providing true justice for their legal claims (2 Sam 15:1–6). He persuades his audience with his rhetoric and causes them to shift their allegiance to Absalom's cause.[84] After driving David from his throne with the assistance of his chief adviser and co-conspirator, Ahithophel, Absalom moves to play his advisers off each other. In the end, he silences his truly wise counselor in favor of someone (David's counterspy, Hushai) whose flowery rhetoric gives him the advice he wants to hear (17:7–13). Ahithophel then commits suicide realizing his voice will no longer be heard in Absalom's court (17:23).[85] It is ironic that Absalom, who came to power through demagoguery, is then undermined and set on the path to his death by a speaker who employs some of the same rhetorical strategies.

A recognized leader provides direction to his followers, and that can include the command that they be silent. Thus, Moses assesses his authority by telling the Israelites to "keep still" as they stood precariously between the Red Sea and the approaching forces of the Egyptian pharaoh (Exod 14:13–14). The respect that he is due as their newly recognized leader rests on the people's willingness to set aside their fear and allow "the Lord to fight for you." In such a situation, it takes real courage and absolute faith to stand fast without panicking and trust in YHWH to act on their behalf.[86] He and the Levitical priests sum up and officially sanction the legal pronouncements that they have given to the people. Using a word for silence that appears nowhere else in the Bible, these religious leaders call for the full attention of the people so that they are fully aware of the momentous charge they have been given.[87] Their obedient silence in this instance expresses their assent and willingness to obey the Lord's commandments (Deut 27:9–10).

Calling for silence likely depends on the faith that the people have in their leader. Joshua, in preparation for the siege of Jericho, instructs the Israelites "You shall not shout or let your voice be heard, nor shall you utter a word until the day I tell you to shout" (Josh 6:10). Like Moses's call to "be still" and await YHWH's intervention at the Red Sea, Joshua's command must have confused the people of Jericho. Processing in ritual silence (or at least wordlessness) around the city for six days could have unnerved them. It also took the strong will of Joshua's leadership and the willingness of the Israelites to participate in what may have seemed a futile exercise. Still, the Israelites will repeatedly fight at the behest of YHWH the Divine Warrior and those designated by divine command to lead them.[88] By commanding silence Joshua demonstrates how he and the Israelites can destroy without uttering words or curses.[89] He increases his own authority as both a military leader and as the agent of YHWH while effectively "quieting" a major city along the conquest route.[90]

Not everyone who hears this calming promise of divine help can accept it without question and remain silent. King Ahaz of Judah receives similar advice from Isaiah as Jerusalem prepares for a siege by the forces of Israel and Aram. The prophet instructs him to "be quiet, do not fear" and "stand firm in faith" during this political crisis (Isa 7:4, 9b). In this case, the king is commanded to remain passive based on his faith in YHWH to manage the situation.[91] Ahaz cannot summon the courage to accept what to him must have seemed an impossible message. He makes an alliance with the Assyrians (2 Kgs 16:7–9) that will haunt him and his successor Hezekiah, fulfilling the rest of Isaiah's prophecy of approaching famine, impoverishment, and destruction (Isa 7:14–25).

Diplomatic affairs can be tricky, and they require careful orchestration and adherence to a set of protocols designed to make official

communications clear to the nations involved so that honor is maintained and treaty arrangements remain intact.[92] Public rituals acknowledging the covenant relationship between the two nations are typical
prior to the submission of a royal message and negotiations, if necessary,
commence. Of course, that message goes through channels before it
reaches the king and that can lead to misunderstandings.[93] An example
of how this process can be subverted is found when the advisers to
King Hanun of Ammon place a very different spin on David's sending
a delegation to the king (2 Sam 10:3). David's purpose, as a covenant
partner, was to have them provide expressions of condolence after the
death of the previous king. They may also have intended to participate
in mourning rituals. However, the Ammonite advisers suggest that
David has sent these men on a spy mission, and they convince the newly
crowned king to respond in a very undiplomatic way. He has David's
men seized and humiliated in a manner that effectively emasculates
them.[94] David's messengers have half of their beards shaved off and a
portion of their garments are cut away, revealing their buttocks and
genitalia (2 Sam 10:4).

Shaming emissaries is equivalent to shaming the ruler who sent
them.[95] If this violent response to David's delegates took place in public
before representatives from other nations, their shaming is that much
more acute and will require a suitable reaction on David's part.[96] Still,
David, before taking the field against Ammon and their Aramaean
allies (2 Sam 10:6), must first rectify the insult to his men and himself.
He physically silences them by sequestering them in Jericho until their
beards grow back (10:5). Taking them out of the public's view makes
this "statement" by the Ammonite king ineffective. Silencing in this
case involves removing both the insult and the possibility of speech by
the delegates.

It is extremely important for a king during a crisis to be able to
shape the official message, and that can include commanding silence
from his close advisers in diplomatic situations.[97] If they attempt to
stretch their instructions to include their own ideas, that can diminish
the king's authority and his strategy in dealing with foreign rulers. For

that reason, Hezekiah orders his representatives to keep silent in the face of the harsh demands expressed by the Assyrian diplomat, the Rabshakeh, during the 701 BCE siege of Jerusalem (2 Kgs 18:36).[98] Hezekiah's advisers are sent to hear the Assyrian's speech, since it would not follow diplomatic protocol for the king to speak in person to the Assyrian king's representative. The king's officials would find this order to stand silent uncomfortable. They must listen without making any rejoinder to the Assyrian ambassador's taunting speech and his use of prophetic illusions.[99]

Worst of all the ambassador speaks in Hebrew. Everyone within earshot on the walls of Jerusalem would be able to understand his words (2 Kgs 18:19–25, 28–35). Hezekiah realized that any response by the king's advisers that did not come directly from him would undermine his attempt to put on a show of defiance to the Assyrians during the siege.[100] In addition, the king would certainly not wish to acknowledge the Rabshakeh's use of a theodicy that suggests YHWH is complicit in the danger to the city because of Hezekiah's cultic reform and the suppression of local high places (18:4 and 22).[101]

The officials' only attempt to minimize the damage and suppress public reaction to the king occurs when they call on the Assyrian to speak in Aramaic rather than in Hebrew (2 Kgs 18:26). The Rabshakeh instead continues to speak in Hebrew to the people "on the walls" as his purpose is to heighten their fears and end their support of Hezekiah during this crisis (18:28–35).[102] By silencing his officials, whose only task here seems to be to witness and then transmit the Rabshakeh's speech to the king, Hezekiah falls into a diplomatic trap. Silencing in this case weakens the king's stance and ultimately results in stripping Jerusalem of much of its wealth as a ransom for the city (18:14–16).[103]

Silencing also functions as one of the tools employed by the head of an Israelite household. His primary role as the head of the household is to ensure that his household prospers as a social unit within their village. By protecting the household's honor, the father demonstrates its value and right to do business within that community. Solidifying his authority is a set of social controls or protocols that govern behavior and tie members of the household together. That naturally includes controlling their speech. Such restrictions remind members of a household of a set of social expectations based on gender, age, and social status. They also set a tone for how individuals are to interact with the extended range of persons identified as Israelites and those labeled as "strangers" (gerîm).[104]

Silencing within the household is found in the aftermath of Tamar's rape by her half-brother Amnon (2 Sam 13:1–22). Her brother Absalom sternly tells her to be silent and not broadcast any further the violence that had been done to her.[105] Her public cries, her ash filled hair, and the disheveled and torn condition of her distinctive clothing have already served as public signs of her distress and personal loss (13:19). They have broadcast the shaming of Absalom's household, indicating his inability to protect the women under his charge. Now he does not wish for it to be broadcast any further. Absalom knows that her rape is a political act committed by Amnon.[106] He needs time to prepare his challenge and to restore his household's honor, and therefore Tamar must be vocally and mentally muted.[107] Silencing Tamar in fact transforms her into a "null persona" while serving Absalom's purposes, until he can take his revenge two years later (13:23–29).[108]

Silencing as a Sign of Wisdom

A chaotic or dangerous situation may demand a temporary silencing of voices.[109] In biblical wisdom literature that is one of the cardinal definitions of the "wise." Sirach points to a characteristic of the wise person as one who understands when it is best "to keep silent" or to "remain silent until the right moment" (Sir 20:1, 7). Proverbs echoes this sentiment saying that the prudent know when it is best to restrain their desire to speak (Prov 10:19) and even fools are considered wise if they refrain from speaking (17:28). Non-association with "merry-makers" who have no grasp of reality is one of the attributes that Jeremiah cites when he describes the ridicule that he has endured for speaking YHWH's message (Jer 15:15–17).[110]

Amos, recognizing the difficult times in which he prophesies, cautions that "the prudent will keep silent" (Amos 5:13).[111] This may be why Saul decided not to lash out at his detractors and instead remain silent for a time after Samuel revealed him as the chosen king (1 Sam 10:20–27a).[112] Saul had received a mixed reception from the people and knew he would have to demonstrate his abilities if he expected wider acceptance as king.[113] That is then accomplished in his successful campaign to relieve the siege of Jabesh-Gilead (1 Sam 10:27b–11).[114]

One of Job's responses to Zophar contains a litany of YHWH's powers in controlling all things. It refers to YHWH as the one who can build up and tear down with impunity (Job 12:14).[115] He also acknowledges that YHWH is the source of wisdom and strength, the giver of wisdom and the one, who for divine purposes, chooses to silence the "trusted" and "take away the discernment of the elders" (12:20).[116] And yet, as is clear in the prologue to Job, YHWH is quite verbose, and that initiates the dialogue with "the Satan" that leads to Job's "testing."[117]

That is also the conclusion in Lamentations when it admonishes those who have experienced suffering or loss "to wait quietly for the salvation of the Lord" (Lam 3:26–27). There is even reference to YHWH also becoming "calm" and introspective after inflicting harsh punishment on his disobedient and promiscuous wife in Ezekiel's metaphorical tale of the foundling (Ezek 16:42).[118] The admonition in Psalms 4:5 makes this point by cautioning against letting anger lead to sin. It is better to ponder the situation "and be silent."[119]

In public settings, silence is often the proper stance. The Egyptian sage Ptah-hotep counsels that when employed by a powerful patron it is best to "speak only when spoken to" and the Assyrian wisdom figure Ahiqar cautions that one should "guard your tongue" and not engage in gossip as words once released "can never be recaptured."[120] For this same reason the author of Proverbs notes that "wisdom is with the humble" but "even fools who keep silent are considered wise" (Prov 11:12).[121] And Ecclesiastes makes it clear that there is "a time to keep silence and a time to speak" (Eccl 3:7).[122]

CHAPTER FIVE

The Silent God

SILENCE, WHETHER UNEXPECTED or prolonged, is often unnerving. Simply put, humans live in a world of sounds, and when normal or expected sounds are cut off, a range of reactions from fear to relief can occur.[1] The silence of individuals or crowds of people is just as ambiguous as it is ephemeral in nature.[2] When it occurs, the immediate response is to determine its cause, as no silence is considered trivial or unimportant if it is noticeable.[3] Axiomatically, when a god is silent, that silence is open to many different interpretations and can lead to misunderstanding, uncertainty, or even conflict if an explanation is not found or created quickly. Are we being ignored or slighted? Is the deity angry with us or otherwise occupied? The unsettling character of inexplicable or sudden or prolonged silence is the basis for more self-examination, recrimination, or simple frustration than any number of words.

Nevertheless, divine silence is not to be equated with divine absence. If the deity were to be truly absent, that removes divine action from the world and eliminates the possibility for interaction with humanity.[4] It negates the silencing of nature as an indication of YHWH's command over all creation and transforms it into a simple natural phenomenon.[5] In fact, the elements of creation are said to be a daily testament without words to the "glory of God." Their very existence means that there is no need for speech (Ps 19:1–4). Even the pause from one day of creation to the next allows YHWH to certify that each creation is "good," and in that way the silence between creative activity expresses satisfaction (Gen 1:4, 12, 18, 25, 31).[6]

In the biblical world, the assumption is that YHWH may choose to respond or not. And a lack of immediate response does not necessarily mean that no communication has or will occur. Acknowledging the fact that YHWH may decide to "hide himself" (Isa 45:15) provides evidence of YHWH's existence rather than proof of nonexistence.[7] Silence, therefore, can be a powerful form of communication if it is seen as providing the pause to consider both the petition and the expected response.[8] Thus the deity is never totally absent from the people's lives nor refusing to listen to their petitions.[9] That is made clear in the preface to the Exodus story when after many years YHWH "heard" the lament of the Israelites in Egypt and "took notice of them" (Exod 2:23–25).[10]

At the most basic level, human perception of God's absence or presence appears in everyday concerns such as birth, death, and illness, as well as in more global issues like waging war or choosing a king.[11] If prayers remain unanswered, petitioners seek explanations to better understand God's silence or lack of responsiveness.[12] The expectation of a divine response is heightened by those rare instances in the text when YHWH chooses to take the unusual step of speaking to a human (Moses) "face to face" (Exod 33:11).[13] It also becomes the basis for exhorting priests and prophets to continue to "cry out" and intercede with YHWH for the people (1 Sam 7:8).[14]

On those occasions when God is silent for a long time, concerns, even anguish, may be raised among the faithful about the meaning of this period of silence. Are there simply times, historical periods, or cultural settings when YHWH is obviously noncommunicative? That is the case in the transitionary period between the Judges Period and the beginning of the monarchy. Regarding that period, the author of 1 Samuel notes that "the word of the Lord was rare in those days; visions were not widespread" (1 Sam 3:1). Of course, this statement is a preface to the call of Samuel, but it is also an acknowledgment by the biblical writer that communication with YHWH had its low points, especially when the religious leadership (Eli) was lacking in its perception of YHWH's will.[15]

The psalmist provides a reaction to the apparent silence of YHWH asking, "Will you forget me forever?" (Ps 13:1).[16] This concern then results in prayers of supplication, calling on God not to remain silent

(39:12–13). Nevertheless, there is still an assumption here that if God "does not answer" immediately (22:2) there remains an expectation that communication between God and human beings remains a real possibility.[17] Otherwise, there would be no point for the psalmist to call out "do not refuse to hear me" or be deaf to my plea "like those who go down to the Pit" (28:1). This petition is based on the belief that if YHWH chooses not to listen, then there is no hope since divine action is the only solution.[18] Furthermore, it encourages Israel's enemies to speak and act more boldly against them.[19]

The psalmist makes it clear that the effort to address God is not a wasted effort (Ps 5:1) and trust is still present based on YHWH's "steadfast love" (13:5).[20] Despite the apparent prosperity of the wicked and one's own bitterness, there are times when the petitioner chooses to remain silent (39:2–3; 73:15–16).[21] Still, assurance is given that YHWH will "hold my right hand" and provide wise counsel to overcome my own arrogance (73:22–28). Within this self-assurance is a growing understanding that silence itself is a communicative act. It is one that needs to be interpreted individually based on the context.[22] YHWH's silence even serves as a modeling of proper behavior when the petitioner realizes that attentive silence is another way to invite speech.[23]

The mourning rituals of Job's three "friends," who come to comfort him in his troubles include crying aloud, tearing their clothing, and throwing dust into the air over their heads.[24] These expressions of grief are followed by the trio sitting with him for seven days in silence (Job 2:11–13). Their actions may function as a sign of solidarity with the sufferer, who is at the brink of death. In performing this ritual act, they affirm that one can only be rescued from that state by God.[25] Sufferers often find that enduring their condition is aided by the mere presence of others. In this way, the three friends' shared silence expresses compassion for his lost children and his precarious physical health, and it identifies with the annihilating and gloomy character of death.[26] Unfortunately, it is when they begin to speak that Job's mental and physical suffering takes center stage.

A seven-day pause in which an individual or a group sits in silence can also function as a plea to YHWH for relief or to elicit communication. That is the case when Ezekiel, after his initial call to become a prophet, sits "appalled" for seven days with the exiled Judeans at Tel-abib. The magnitude of the mission placed before him had brought him to this stunned state that compares with the silent despair of the exiles. After resisting his call for seven days, he simply states, "the word of the Lord came to me" (Ezek 3:15–16). Silence in this case may have been preparation for his mission or, alternatively, a form of resistance. In the end, it is the voice of YHWH that commands him to accept his role as a "sentry" and serve as a prophetic spokesperson.[27]

In most cases, the petitioner in individual psalms or in collective laments considers the deity or deities to be a ready communication partner, approachable and capable of listening. The psalmist cries out for YHWH to answer his prayer (Pss 4:1; 13:3; 20:9), for once he departs this life, prayer and praise of the deity stops (Pss 39:12–13; 115:16–18).[28] Death ends all communication with YHWH and any expectation of a response ceases (Ps 6:5).[29] Thus, when attempting to communicate with a god, it is only natural to employ normal social conventions such as opening gestures, turn taking, and polite or deferential addresses.[30] These conventions occur as part of normal social discourse, standard interpersonal interactions and dialogue.[31] When metaphors are employed as part of this communication, they help to illustrate the reduced or threatened state of the petitioner and the gravity of the threat.[32] Frequently, metaphors are designed to elicit an emotional and positive response from the deity.[33]

There are times when the deity does not immediately respond to prayer or supplication despite the poignant case made by the petitioner.[34] The lack of response is sometimes declared to be justified, as it is in the case of the Israelites' rebellion against YHWH after they initially refused to enter the Promised Land (Deut 1:45). Similarly, the prophet Amos points to the unfaithfulness of Israel as the cause of a "famine" of hearing the word of the Lord.[35] No amount of searching will bring it forth or allow them to hear YHWH (Amos 8:11–12).[36] The graphic depiction of the wrath of YHWH that resulted in the utter destruction of Jerusalem and the decimation of its people includes the anguished cry for relief that is left unheard. The supplicant must acknowledge that their punishment is because of the peoples' rejection of God's teachings and their rebellion against his word (Jer 6:19–23; Lam 1:18). YHWH therefore has chosen to "shut out my prayers" (Lam 3:8).[37] The loss of the peoples' fear of YHWH takes on an almost sarcastic tone in Third Isaiah. YHWH says, "Have I not kept silent and closed my eyes, so you do not fear me?" (Isa 57:11–13). Those who have relied on their idols will have their pleas carried away by the wind while only those who take refuge in YHWH will be allowed to possess the land.[38]

Of course, belief in divine presence coupled with prolonged divine silence can result in despair and a sense of abandonment. That emotion is expressed with the mournful question, "Will you forget me forever" (Ps 13:1).[39] There are a variety of explanations when a deity does not speak to the specifics of petitions or complaints. For instance, is God's silence in response to a petition a reflection of an uncaring deity? King Saul faces this question when he is unable to receive a response from God, and that leads him to make rash decisions and, eventually, to take his query to the Witch of Endor (1 Sam 14:37; 28:6). There is no one who feels more isolated than the supplicant whose cry remains unheard.[40]

There is an apparent angst associated with a penitent's unanswered plea when God chooses to remain silent. Most of the examples of this emotional response appear in the Psalms (28:1; 83:2). However, the complaint form appears prominently in Habakkuk (Hab 1:13) where the prophet berates God's failure to respond in a time of crisis despite a previous revelation.[41] In this same vein is the anguished cry of the stricken people after the destruction of Jerusalem by the Babylonians in 587 BCE (Lam 3:8).[42] They feel "cut off" from all communication.

Job's frustration is evident as he curses the day of his birth and in his zeal calls upon a reversal of creation to its primordial state of chaos (Job 3:3–9).[43] His response to his suffering then focuses on his call for YHWH to appear before him and provide a rational explanation

for being "hunted down" by God (9:24; 12:9; 19:6–12).[44] Once Job
has exhausted his pleas, the question is whether YHWH's silence
can contribute to or encourage a sense of personal responsibility or
self-evaluation.[45] Of course, YHWH does eventually respond to Job's
plea but does not explicitly answer Job's question of why he is suffering
(38:1–39:30 and 40:1–41:34). YHWH's response is so magisterial and
humbling that Job's resulting silence during YHWH's diatribe serves
as an acknowledgment of Job's reduced status as he cowers in "dust and
ashes" (42:1–6).[46] In the end, this divine-human dialogue reinforces
the admonition to be introspective (Ps 4:4 and Sir 20:7), cautioning
restraint in speaking when passions are high.[47]

The silent deity may well be attentively listening or may have reason
to keep silent. Silence may even be associated with a divine testing of the
petitioner, probing their heart (Ps 17:3).[48] However, the deity cannot be
coerced into speaking or acting.[49] The covenant theme in the Hebrew
Bible describes a god who freely chooses to establish relationships with
humankind (Gen 15:1; 17:2; Exod 6:2–4; Deut 7:7–9). Clearly members
of that covenantal community can seek out YHWH and expect, but
not demand, a response.[50] Thus, silence or the apparent absence of the
deity is based on human perception and is not a true descriptor of the
god with whom they have a relationship.[51]

Forms of Petition

Penitential prayer, whether silent or aloud, private or public, is worth
a close examination in this context. At its heart, prayer is an attempt
to establish a relationship between the petitioner and the deity by
expressing deep-felt fears and concerns, and identifying those forces
of wickedness that either oppress society in general or the petitioner.[52]
In most cases, prayer in ancient Israel, at least outside the confines of
the sanctuary, was not silent.[53] Ordinarily, the words of the prayer were
to be spoken aloud so that the deity could hear them and then make
a judgment of whether to grant the petition.[54] In public ritual, when
penitential prayer is part of the ceremony, the emotions evoked are

aimed at both the audience and the deity.[55] Of course, prayer can happen anywhere, but when the intent is to come into immediate contact with the deity, the belief is that it will have greater success if spoken aloud and within the vicinity of the "home" of the god.[56]

Hannah's silent prayer before the Shiloh sanctuary follows at least a portion of the protocol described above. But her silent plea for a child matched with a vow for the child's future is unique and appears nowhere else in the Hebrew Bible (1 Sam 1:10–13).[57] It is therefore possible to say that when she opens her heart while silently expressing her vow, she is engaging in an unprecedented action while her humble stance makes her a model supplicant.[58] At the same time, she expresses, even silently, her assurance and assertiveness in addressing the deity.[59]

If Hannah's "silent prayer" is indeed a deviation from normal practice, it follows that it is not beyond the bounds to say that Eli is justifiably confused.[60] However, Eli's misunderstanding also leads to his summary attempt to shame and silence her (1 Sam 1:14). His lack of perception and his effort to exercise his authority as the guardian officiant at the shrine at Shiloh gives more credence to the emotional plea of a humble and childless woman and allows for YHWH to take charge of the situation. Hannah easily clears her name and turns the tables on Eli by her respectful reply to his accusations of her drunkenness (1:15–16).[61] Perhaps recognizing that he has placed himself in a dishonorable position in a place in which he is the gatekeeper and chief official, Eli is quick to bless her vow and assure her that YHWH would hear her plea (1:17).[62] And, when her petition is granted by the birth of her son Samuel, Hannah voices a prayer of thanksgiving (2:1–10), completing the cycle of plea, expression of loyalty, and subsequent song of praise found in several individual psalms (Pss 10; 22; 116).[63]

Is remaining silent in the face of trial or suffering an invitation for God to join a conversation with the worshipper?[64] When vocalized penitential prayer and divination are not employed, there is evidence in the text that silence is a means of addressing the deity as a demonstration of faith and an expectation that YHWH already knows what is needed (Ps 62:5–7).[65] One way that the psalmist expresses this concept is in the admonition to remain still before YHWH and "wait patiently for him" (37:7). Silent patience then becomes a form of wisdom instruction that advocates for a life of "pious practice" by those identified as "the poor." This applies not just within a social category but rather for all whose lives are touched by tragedy, oppression, and need (37:12–15).[66]

To "be still and know that I am God" (Ps 46:10), while addressed to enemy nations, provides an assurance to the Israelites of their God's presence and active protection.[67] On another level it allows the meditative believer to set aside emotional distress, retreat from worldly trouble, and seek to achieve a calm spirit.[68] And, obtaining the feeling of contentment experienced by a trusting child, "I do not occupy my mind with things too great and too marvelous for me . . . I have calmed and quieted my soul" (131:1–2).[69] Similarly, that mindset of calm assurance appears in the stalwart statement, "For God alone my soul waits in silence" (62:2, 5). Even though God has not yet addressed or relieved one's troubles, it is possible to patiently wait on YHWH to respond.[70] In that way, YHWH can be praised continuously "in silence" (65:2).

In addition to individual prayers, the ancient Israelites repeatedly employed an official form of divination using the *Urim* and *Thummim* to obtain a yes or no response from YHWH on matters that concern the entire community. The difficulty arises when the response is negative or when there is no definitive response at all. One interpretation of this null response is that God has chosen to evade the question or the person asking the question. Even though no words have been spoken by the deity, the lack of an answer is on par with a spoken reply.[71] That lack of a response can lead to unwise decisions. For example, when an unnerved Saul no longer receives a divine response either through prophet or dreams, he feels it is necessary to go to the Witch of Endor, who employs necromancy as an unsanctioned means of communicating with the spirit of Samuel.[72]

Unfortunately, the text only mentions the *Urim* and *Thummim* ten times and in no instance provides a clear description of their function. All that is stated in the text about them is that they were to be stored in the breastplate of the high priest (Exod 28:30; Lev 8:8). The assumption is that they were a type of lot that could be cast before the assembled people and thus provide an answer to the poised question.[73] That is the case when Joshua is chosen to succeed Moses. Eleazar the high priest is instructed by Moses at YHWH's command to "inquire for him by the decision of the Urim before the Lord" to confirm this appointment (Num 27:21).[74] Whatever their shape or decoration, it is their function as a form of silent communication that is most important here. Perhaps because this divination method does not always provide a clear divine response (1 Sam 28:6), their importance is superseded or replaced when YHWH raises up prophets to speak aloud the deity's message and warnings.

Communication between the people and the deity often is filtered through divination practices, the prophets, priests, or kings. Although YHWH seldom directly addressed the common people, they maintained the expectation that communication is possible and ongoing. Certainly, the theophanic narratives in which a prophet is called by YHWH reiterate that message, and they remind the people that God chooses to speak (Isa 6; Jer 1:4–19; Ezek 1–3:11). To an extent, that expectation is also based on a personal relationship with the deity that begins at birth and remains a reality throughout life. As it is articulated in Psalms 22:10–11, the assumption is that YHWH is ever present at a successful birth and continues to be available for petitions during times of trouble.[75] For that reason, amidst the mocking of others and the penitent's personal pain and suffering, there is reassurance that YHWH remains "my God," always addressable under any circumstance (Ps 22:1–2).[76]

Forms of Divine Response

In what form does a god respond and what is then to be considered a definitive response by the deity? Among the most powerful combinations of divine presence and divine speech occur during a theophany. That is the case when Moses encounters the burning bush (Exod 3:2–4) or when the assembled Israelites stand at the base of Mt. Horeb and hear YHWH's voice booming out of the fire that is blazing up from the mountaintop (Deut 4:11–12; 5:22). The disembodied voice that represents the glory of the deity adds to the mystery of YHWH's person and generates fear among Israel's enemies, making them easy prey in battle (1 Sam 7:10).[77]

YHWH's voice calls on a succession of prophets to begin their ministry and announce the word of the Lord (Num 12:6) and repeatedly transmits the message that the people have failed to obey that divine voice (Jer 9:13; 42:13; Zeph 3:2). Dreams and visions are also associated with the divine voice and serve as a form of divination that provides an indication of YHWH's intentions, whether for a battle (Judg 7:13–14) or some other event of importance (1 Kgs 3:5–14).[78] They can function as an initial call to serve, although some may not be understood until a third party provides instruction (Samuel and Eli in 1 Sam 3:3–14).[79] In some cases they provide a prophetic warning (Jeremiah in Jer 27:9–10), although it is always best to be careful how a question is framed and how it is answered (Micaiah in 1 Kgs 22:19–23).[80] Furthermore, YHWH's ability to speak and interact with creation and the people is made clear by the psalmist who ridicules the idols made of silver and gold that cannot speak, hear, smell, or touch (Ps 115:3–7).[81]

YHWH's voice is often described as thunderously powerful, having a visual impact on the natural world: breaking the cedar trees, flashing with fire, shaking the wilderness, and unleashing the winds (Ps 18:13; 29:3–9; Jer 51:16).[82] In fact, hearing the voice of God as it emerges from fire and thick darkness is a frightening thing that some believe would certainly result in death (Deut 5:24–26 [20–23]; 18:24–26).[83] Throughout the biblical account, a common way of describing the voice of God is as thunder (Exod 19:19; Job 37:2–5; Ezek 1:24), intimidating in its volume and might (1 Sam 7:10; Sir 46:17), and a phenomenon of nature that expresses presence without expressing a specific message.

The sheer number of occasions when YHWH's voice is heard makes those times when it is silent even more startling.[84] For instance, there are occasions when a prophet is surprised that YHWH has not disclosed information that would be crucial to him.[85] In the story of Elisha and

the barren Shunammite woman (2 Kgs 4:8–37), the prophet predicts
the birth of a son even though her husband is old (4:15–16).[86] Elisha's
authority is reinforced when she does give birth to a son, but later in the
tale the child appears to have a seizure and is apparently dead (4:17–19).
His mother saddles a donkey and goes off in search of Elisha, when
placing the boy on Elisha's bed does not suffice to revive him (4:20–25).
Curiously, Elisha first sends his servant Gehazi to speak with the woman
but then relents and asks about the source of her distress (4:25b–27).
At that point, Elisha acknowledges that the fate of the child has been
"hidden" from him by YHWH (4:27).[87] That acknowledgment fits
into a criticism of the prophet for overstepping his abilities, not asking
YHWH what had happened, and putting Elisha in his place.[88] The
narrative does conclude with the resuscitation of the child and a recer-
tification of the prophet's authority (4:29–37), but in this case YHWH
chooses to use silence to instruct a presumptuous and not always reliable
servant.[89]

Silence also appears as a factor in the four servant songs of Second
Isaiah although they contrast with each other in terms of the use of
speech. In the first and fourth the servant does not speak, while the
middle two songs contain a very vocal servant who is empowered and
capable of speaking rightly about YHWH (see Isa 49:1–6 and 50:4–9).
In the first song, there is a silent Israel-as-servant: "He will not cry or
lift up his voice or make it heard in the street" (42:2).[90] In the final song,
there is a shift to a silent prophet-as-servant whose silence is paralleled
with his being "exalted." That then leads to a reversal on the part of the
kings who have oppressed him and whose mouths shall be shut because
of him (52:15): "He was oppressed and he was afflicted, yet he opened
not his mouth; like a lamb that is led to the slaughter, and like a sheep
that is dumb, so he opened not his mouth" (53:7). A final reversal is not
complete until Israel, the powerless nation, finally is able to speak (54:1,
4, 17). The absence of speech in this fourth servant song reinforces the
servant figure's total powerlessness.[91]

Adding to the value of silence here is the frequent repetition of the
command to "hear" or to "listen," especially "Listen to me in silence"

(Isa 41:1).[92] In that way, the penitent takes the time to be introspective, holding to the assurance that YHWH is present (Ps 46:10–11) and will answer when the time is right (50:3). Qoheleth adds a cultic tone to this admonition not to engage in the "sacrifice of fools," but instead "draw near to listen" when intending to go in reverence to the temple (Eccl 5:1).[93]

When Silence is Communication

As noted above, silence is not always a refusal or a failure to communicate.[94] It is also in the power of a deity to address a person through silence or by creating a "heavenly calm."[95] Sometimes, as Eliphaz tells Job, silence is the preface to divine communication that manifests initially as a subtle "whisper" (Job 4:12–16).[96] Job's response (26:5–14) acknowledges YHWH's magisterial control over all of creation, both violent and beautiful. However, he also compares the unfathomable character of divine thunder with "the small whisper" of what humanity hears and understands of God's ways.[97]

Perhaps the best example of divine silence with a purpose or function is found in Elijah's theophany at Mt. Horeb (1 Kgs 19:11–13).[98] As he cowers in a mountain cave, Elijah first experiences the typical manifestations of divine power and control over creation: thunder, wind, and earthquake.[99] After all the commotion within the natural world ends, Elijah is then said to perceive YHWH's presence in "a sound of sheer silence."[100] The contrast between the cacophony of sounds and the abrupt silence sets the stage for divine speech and draws Elijah's attention closer to what will be said.[101] Such an extraordinary occurrence goes beyond the norm as it is practically impossible to experience true silence.[102] Even in those circumstances in which there is a complete absence of movement to disturb the air, we still note some sound, however faint.[103] Furthermore, a particular silence may not simply represent the total absence of sound but rather function as the absence of a particular sound.[104]

In this way, silence on Mt. Horeb becomes the true sign of God's presence and attentiveness to the prophet.[105] When Elijah is instructed to leave his cave of concealment and stand upon the mountainside, he experiences some of the typical manifestations of a theophany: strong winds, earthquake, and fire (1 Kgs 19:11–12a).[106] Once all the physical signs have quieted down, Elijah at last perceives God's true presence in "a sound of sheer silence" (19:12b).[107] Aside from exploring what is meaningful here is a discussion of the "absence of sound" or an absence of a particular or expected sound.[108] In that way, expectation is raised, and the reader or audience holds its breath just as Job does in preparation for a divine pronouncement. Attendant to this example are instances in which God "silences" normal sounds to provide a space in which to manifest divine power (Isa 24:8; 25:5; 32:8).[109]

The theophany on Mt. Horeb stands in stark contrast to the events described when Elijah challenges the 450 prophets of Ba'al to a public contest on Mt. Carmel (1 Kgs 18:19). The stated aim is to end a three-year drought that had resulted in a devastating famine (18:2). Theologically, such a contest should assist the Ba'al prophets. Their deity, once arisen from his temporary "death" during the dry months of the summer, could be roused to bring the lifegiving rains during the fall and winter months.[110] The Carmel mountains serve as the highest point looking westward into the Mediterranean Sea. They function as the perfect weather station to glimpse an approaching storm front, and their projecting peaks cause the rain-bringing westerly winds to drop moisture that can transform the slopes and nearby area into an Eden-like agricultural zone.[111] As the narrative progresses, it will become clear that Ba'al's attributes as a storm god cannot serve as an alternative or match for YHWH's power over all creation.[112] In fact, it is only YHWH's presence, exemplified by the thunder and lightning, that provides what the people truly need while Ba'al's absence proves to be immaterial.[113]

Before beginning the contest, Elijah calls on the people to choose between YHWH and Ba'al, but "the people did not answer him a word" (1 Kgs 18:21). The people's silence is their way of avoiding a direct response, choosing instead to await the result of the demonstration of divine power that Elijah then proposes.[114] Elijah gives the Ba'al prophets the opportunity to build an altar and sacrifice a bull and then call out to Ba'al (18:25). The contest between them is designed to see whose god would choose to manifest in power when called upon by their prophet(s). At stake is proof of divine existence or at least proof of a willingness to interact with worshippers.

When Ba'al's voice provides no answer or evidence of his presence, the prophets redouble their efforts. They call on their god and engage in a "limping" dance around the altar that is designed to focus their minds on the divine plain and attract the attention of Ba'al. In extremis, they also cut themselves, miming the sacrifice offered to their god (1 Kgs 18:26, 28–29). All this time Elijah stands back, mocking the Ba'al prophets, asking them if he is "meditating," "gone on a journey," or "asleep" (18:27).[115] This latter accusation (asleep) refers to an inactive deity who cannot or does not choose to respond to his worshippers' summons.[116] Concern over a similar, unresponsive divine attitude is found in the petition of the psalmist who calls on YHWH to "rouse yourself, why do you sleep" . . . "Why do you hide your face" (Ps 44:23–24).[117] In response to this concern, the psalmist also refers to YHWH as the one who is always vigilant and "neither slumbers nor sleeps" (121:3–4). Ever alert, YHWH is characterized as the sovereign over creation whose control is absolute and unchallenged by the elements of chaos.[118]

Elijah's taunting of the Ba'al prophets is just as much an accusation against their god, who, despite all their frenzied efforts, provides them with a null response.[119] When the voice of Ba'al is not heard, that indicates a lack of action as well as divine indifference. Either serves the purposes of Elijah's challenge; proving that YHWH really is the God who acts. YHWH's absence during the three-year drought adds suspense to the story. When Elijah calls out his invocation, YHWH reveals his divine presence in dramatic fashion. YHWH consumes both altars on Mt. Carmel as well as the trench filled with water that divides them like the waters of creation (1 Kgs 18:32–38). The people who are witnessing these events then fall on their faces in awe. They profess their faith in YHWH and follow this act of worship with a murderous frenzy that includes the slaughter of the Ba'al prophets (18:39–40). In this way, Ba'al, who has remained a silent god, is joined in his silence by the silencing of his prophets. And the rain, when it comes, provides a final crescendo to these events (18:45).

* * *

Silence, when associated with the deity, immediately draws attention to itself. The ancient Near Eastern world included competing gods and religions as part of the political and social compass. No nation discounted the importance of their gods, and all attempted to discover the will of the gods who created the world and managed its affairs. When communication with the divine ceased, even temporarily, it signaled the need to find the meaning for this silence and determine what needed to be done to placate or restore the relationship with the gods. As a result, divination methods were developed and prophets were called to provide the message of the god(s). Sacrifices were made and cultic rituals were performed to honor the gods and either bring needed blessings (rain, good harvests, military victories) or to prevent the gods from punishing the people for their unfaithfulness or neglect of divine injunctions.

The ancient Israelites participated in many of these same practices, but they also developed a religious system that privileged a single deity and eventually evolved a monotheistic belief. That meant that when YHWH was silent, they could not simply attempt to invoke another god. Greater attention to the voice of YHWH found in their obligation to the law and the covenant was necessary. Failure to listen to prophetic warnings could put a punctuation mark to their relationship with YHWH. When disobedience and concern for personal gain or advancement became a hindrance to listening to YHWH's voice (Ps 81:8–13; 95:7b–11), the Israelites were compelled to accept the theodicy of deserved punishment outlined by the prophets.[120] That gave them the opportunity to become more attentive listeners, giving a temporarily silent YHWH the opportunity to speak to them once again and reengage what had begun with YHWH speaking first to Abram (Gen 12:1), and eventually to the nation as a whole (Ps 50:3–6).[121]

NOTES

CHAPTER ONE

1. Ana Dragojlovic and Annemarie Samuels, "Tracing Silences: Towards an Anthropology of the Unspoken and Unspeakable," *History & Anthropology* 32, no. 4 (2021): 417.

2. Isabella van Elferen and Sven Raeymaekers, "Silent Dark: The Orders of Silence," *Journal for Cultural Research* 19, no. 3 (2015): 262.

3. Graham Turner, *The Power of Silence: The Riches That Lie Within* (New York: Bloomsbury, 2012), 1.

4. Robin Reames, "Speech in Pursuit of Silence," *Philosophy & Rhetoric* 55/1 (2022): 33, refers to the "silence of asceticism" as internalized speech. It can be compared to the silent prayer.

5. Victor H. Matthews, *More Than Meets the Ear: Discovering the Hidden Contexts of Old Testament Conversations* (Grand Rapids, MI: Eerdmans, 2008), 68–70.

6. Izydora Dambska, "Silence as an Expression and as a Value," in *Knowledge, Language and Silence: Selected Papers*, eds. Anna Brozek and Jacek Jadacki (Leiden: Brill, 2016), 312–313.

7. Bernard P. Dauenhauer, *Silence: The Phenomenon and Its Ontological Significance* (Bloomington, IN: Indiana University Press, 1980), 55, characterizes this as employing "abstinence," rather than attempting to say or do something beyond your abilities or knowledge.

8. Dambska, "Silence as an Expression and as a Value," 312.

9. Wayne C. Booth, *The Knowing Most Worth Doing* (Charlottesville, VA: University of Virginia Press, 2010), 77.

10. Monica B. Vieira, "Representing Silence in Politics," *American Political Science Review* 114, no. 4 (2020): 977–979.

11. Cheryl Glenn, *Unspoken: A Rhetoric of Silence* (Carbondale, IL: Southern Illinois University Press, 2004), 10.

12. Reames, "Speech in Pursuit of Silence," 33.
13. Kris Acheson, "Silence as Gesture: Rethinking the Nature of Communicative Silences," *Communication Theory* 18, no. 4 (2008): 552.
14. van Elferen and Raeymaekers, "Silent Dark," 265, calls this form of mental gymnastics "silence by negation."
15. Mark G. Brett. "Abraham's 'Heretical' Imperative: A Response to Jacques Derrida," in *Meanings We Choose* (London; New York: T&T Clark, 2004), 168, n. 12, argues that "editorial intention is a useful shorthand for speaking about the historical agency that may lie behind the making of the 'final' text."
16. Wayne C. Booth, "Where is the Authorial Audience in Biblical Narrative—and in Other 'Authoritative' Texts?" *Narrative* 4/3 (1996): 235–236.
17. Wayne C. Booth, *The Rhetoric of Fiction*, 2nd ed. (Chicago: University of Chicago Press, 1983), 303, states that "there are many things a reader can be asked to do besides guessing about who is doing what to whom or about whether it is good or bad that he does so."
18. Susan L. Graham, "On Scripture and Authorial Intent: A Narratological Proposal," *Anglican Theological Review* 77/3 (1995): 307–320.
19. David Hayman, *Ulysses: The Mechanics of Meaning* (Englewood Cliffs, NJ: Prentice-Hall, 1970), 70.
20. See the analysis of the Dtr compilation of the Former Prophets in which "traditions serve scribes" in K. L. Noll, "A Portrait of the Deuteronomistic Historian at Work?" in *Raising Up a Faithful Exegete: Essays in Honor of Richard D. Nelson*, eds. K. L. Noll and Brooks Schramm (Winona Lake, IN: Eisenbrauns, 2010), 73–86.
21. Meindert Dijkstra, "'As for the other events . . .': Annals and Chronicles in Israel and the Ancient Near East," in *The Old Testament in Its World* (Leiden; Boston: Brill, 2005), 14–44.
22. Lewis A. Lawson, "Walker Percy's Silent Character," *The Mississippi Quarterly* 33/2 (1980), 123.
23. Susan S. Lanser, *The Narrative Act: Point of View in Prose Fiction* (Princeton, NJ: Princeton University Press, 1981), 53.
24. Jerome Bruner, "The Narrative Construction of Reality," *Critical Inquiry* 18 (1991): 4–5.
25. There are occasional references to silence in the New Testament where appropriate.
26. That may explain why Psalm 50:3 is so adamant that "our God comes and does not keep silence."

CHAPTER TWO

1. Restricting characters and their speech in this way can be jarring to the modern reader, who is remote from the culture and world of the original or "authorial audience." Peter Rabinowitz, *Before Reading: Narrative Conventions and the Politics of Interpretation* (Ithaca: Cornel University Press, 1987), 36–42, outlines the difficulties of "authorial reading" and the ambiguity that is created when the "reader's starting point" and that of the text/story do not match.

2. Wayne C. Booth, "The Ethics of Teaching Literature," in *The Essential Wayne Booth,* ed. Walter Jost (Chicago: University of Chicago Press, 2006), 236, citing Rabinowitz, *Before Reading,* 29–36, refers to them as the "authorial audience" who are "aware that a 'made-up' story is being told" but "shares with the implied author at least a fair number of basic assumptions about life and its realities."

   Booth, "The Ethics of Teaching Literature," 230; and Wayne C. Booth, "Where is the Authorial Audience in Biblical Narrative?" *Narrative* 4, no. 3 (1996): 237, points to the difficulties faced of an audience that is remote from the culture that produced an ancient story. They may fail to employ the skills that "the original authors may well have assumed."

3. Victor H. Matthews and Don C. Benjamin, "Stories of Gilgamesh," in *Old Testament Parallels: Laws and Stories form the Ancient Near East,* 5th ed. (Mahwah, NJ: Paulist, 2023), 41–54.

4. William O. Beeman, "Silence in Music," in *Silence: The Currency of Power,* ed. Maria-Luisa Achino-Loeb (New York: Berghahn Books, 2006), 23, describes how a composition with continuous sound buries the richer elements of a composition.

   Graham Turner, *The Power of Silence: The Riches That Lie Within* (New York: Bloomsbury, 2012), 47.

5. Walter J. Ong, *Orality and Literacy: The Technologizing of the Word* (London: Routledge, 2002), 38–40, characterizes an oral society as one that requires redundancy for speaker and hearer to remain on track and part of the oration. Even in an acoustically difficult setting, repetition keeps the audience engaged and able to participate. And one wonders why no reference is made regarding God's decision to spare Noah and his family after determining that Noah was the only righteous person in all the world (Gen 6:1–8).

6. Four hundred shekels of silver is exorbitant. Nathan MacDonald, "Driving a Hard Bargain? Genesis 23 and Models of Economic Exchange," in *Anthropology and Biblical Studies: Avenues of Approach,*

eds. Louise J. Lawrence and Mario Aquilar (Leiden: Deo, 2004), 90–96, points to the difficulties of employing "cross-cultural models of economic exchange" to interpret a biblical narrative. He sees the exchange between Abraham and Ephron as an example of "negative reciprocity," which frees Abraham from any future economic or social obligation to the seller. Still, it is interesting that Ephron does not employ the legal ruse of adopting Abraham into his household and instead agrees to an outright sale of land.

7. The need for a title to the land is then reiterated in Jeremiah's redemption of his family's property during the last days of Judah's existence as an independent nation (Jer 32:1–15).

8. See Carrie Cifers, "She Decides: Reading Genesis 34 in Conversation with Narrative Ethics," *Interpretation* 77, no. 1 (2023): 59, for a discussion of "withholding information" by the narrator and a reference to this practice in Leona Toker, *Eloquent Reticence: Withholding Information in Fictional Narrative* (Lexington, KY: U. Press of Kentucky, 2014), 5–6.

9. Maria-Luisa Achino-Loeb, "Introduction," in *Silence: The Currency of Power*, edited by Maria-Luisa Achino-Loeb (New York: Berghahn Books, 2006), 2–3, ties silence to a means of forging identity, a practice that is certainly at play in the Abraham narrative.

10. R. Christopher Heard, *Dynamics of Diselection: Ambiguity in Genesis 12–36 and Ethnic Boundaries in Post-Exilic Judah* (Semeia 39; Atlanta: SBL, 2001), 183–184, points to a series of "dis-elections" in which marginal characters such as Lot, Eliezer, and Ishmael are excluded from the covenant promise.

11. For additional usage of this phrase as a narrative link, see Genesis 15:1; 22:20; Joshua 24:29; Ezra 9:1; Esther 2:1; 3:1. Shimon Bar-Efrat, *Narrative Art in the Bible* (Sheffield, England: Almond Press, 1989), 133, notes a similar opening phrase "and after this" as a narrative connector in 2 Sam 13:1 and 15:1.Unlike Job's self-assurance (Job 23:10), Abraham does not seem to be aware he is being tested. He is only following a divine command.

12. Don C. Benjamin, *The Old Testament Story, an Introduction* (Minneapolis: Fortress, 2004), 65–68, frames this as a form of training rather than testing. While it has the marks of an ordeal, its purpose is to train the Israelites to meet challenges, and the ordeal that Abraham must endure serves as a clarification of the covenant promise.Christo Lambard, "Testing Tales: Genesis 22 and Daniel 3 and 6," in *Prayers and the Construction of Israelite Identity*, eds. Susanne Gillmayr-Bucher

and Maria Häusl (Atlanta: SBL, 2019), 115–117, sees Gen 22:1b and 22:15–18 as editorial additions to the original story serving the theological purpose of encouraging the audience to also have "blind trust in all circumstances."

13. For a similar case of "testing" see 2 Chr 32:31 (with the fuller story in 2 Kgs 20:12–19) in which God tests Hezekiah "to know all that was in his heart."

14. Mark G. Brett, *Genesis: Procreation and the Politics of Identity* (London: Routledge, 2000), 73, points out that Abraham does not know he is being tested. The narrator has only told the audience.

15. See how this story compares to a similar, unprompted command by Artemis in the Hesiod version of the Iphigenia story in Raleigh C. Heth, "Isaac and Iphigenia: Portrayals of Child Sacrifice in Israelite and Greek Literature," *Bib* 104, no. 2 (2021): 481–502.

16. See the contributions on the traditional readings of the Akedah in Judaism, Christianity, and Islam in Bradley Beach and Matthew T. Powell, eds. *Interpreting Abraham: Journeys to Moriah* (Minneapolis: Fortress, 2014). See Ethan Schwartz, "The Theological Pretension of the Ethical: Reframing the Jewish Significance of Genesis 22," *Int* 77, no. 1 (2023): 40–51. Also note Jacques Derrida, *A Taste for the Secret* (Cambridge: Polity Press, 2001), 67, who characterizes Abraham's total allegiance to what he calls the "absolute other" that "propels him into the space or risk of absolute sacrifice."

17. This literary device is quite common. See Genesis 27:1; 31:11; 37:13; 46:2; Exodus 3:4 among other instances.

18. Robert L. Scott, "Dialectical Tensions of Speaking and Silence," *Quarterly Journal of Speech* 79, no. 1 (1993): 10, ties this form of silence as a response to the "structure of privilege" in a society that requires or expects silence in socially governed situations. That position works well with the admonition in Psalm 46:10, "Be still, and know that I am God!"

19. Robert Crotty, "The Literary Structure of the Binding of Isaac in Genesis 22," *ABR* 53 (2005): 31.

20. Wayne C. Booth, *The Knowing Most Worth Doing* (Charlottesville: U. of Virginia Press, 2010), 77, notes that "It should be obvious that no readers will ever be interested in a text that does not in some way close off an infinite number of trivial possibilities, in order to open up a relatively small number of significant possibilities."

21. Booth, "The Ethics of Forms," in Walter Jost, ed. *The Essential Wayne Booth* (Chicago: University of Chicago Press, 2006), 213.

22. Richard L. Johannesen, "The Functions of Silence: A Plea for Communication Research," *Western Speech* 38, no. 1 (1974): 29–30. He goes on to catalog potential meanings for silence based on "the backgrounds of the participants, the occasion, and the verbal and nonverbal contexts surrounding the silence."

23. Genesis 22:2.

24. Mark G. Brett, "Abraham's 'Heretical' Imperative: A Response to Jacques Derrida," in *The Meanings We Choose: Hermeneutical Ethics, Indeterminacy and the Conflict of Interpretations*, ed. Charles H. Cosgrove (London: T&T Clark, 2004), 169–170, suggests that the use of this terminology for Isaac permits the narrator to displace the narrator of Genesis 21 and thereby ignore Ishmael's existence altogether.

25. The issue of whether this story provides a precedent of eliminating human sacrifice among the Israelites does not correlate with the fact that they continued to engage in human sacrifice during the monarchy period.
    It continues to appear in moments of crisis, including King Ahaz making "his son pass through the fire" (2 Kgs 16:3) and as a preparation for declaring war against Israel and Aram. Ed Noort, "Genesis 22: Human Sacrifice and Theology in the Hebrew Bible," *The Sacrifice of Isaac: The Aqedah (Genesis 22) and Its Interpretations*, eds. Ed Noort and Eibert Tigchelaar (Leiden: Brill, 2002), 7–8, points to Ezekiel 20:25–26 and Jeremiah 32:35 as indicators of prophetic condemnation of the practice, which continued throughout the monarchy period.

26. Francis Landy, "Narrative Techniques and Symbolic Transactions in the Akedah," in *Signs and Wonders: Biblical Texts in Literary Focus*, ed. J. Cheryl Exum (Atlanta: SBL, 1989), 3.

27. Samuel Terrien, *The Elusive Presence: The Heart of Biblical Theology* (San Francisco: Harper & Row, 1983), 82–83.

28. Omri Boehm, *The Binding of Isaac: A Religious Model of Disobedience* (NY: T&T Clark, 2007), 14–15.

29. Cynthia Miller, "Silence as a Response in Biblical Hebrew," *JNSL* 32, no. 1 (2006): 35. Compare with Genesis 18:6–8 in which Abraham commands Sarah to prepare a meal for his guests, assuming she will carry out these instructions, but the narrative does not contain her response.

30. Brett, "Abraham's 'Heretical' Imperative," 172.

31. J. Aaron Simmons, "What About Isaac? Rereading *Fear and Trembling* and Rethinking Kierkegaardian Ethics," *Journal of Religious Ethics* 35, no. 2 (2007): 336, contends that Abraham's love for Isaac does not need

to be suspended. However, the tension between his love for YHWH and for Isaac forms a key element in the drama.

32. See the examination of the ways that emotions fit Biblical Hebrew experience in Françoise Mirguet, "What is an 'Emotion' in the Hebrew Bible: An Experience that Exceeds Most Contemporary Concepts," *BiBInt* 24, no. 4–5 (2016): 442–465.

33. Paul A. Kruger, "The Face and Emotions in the Hebrew Bible," *OTE* 18, no. 3 (2005): 652, points to the example in the Gilgamesh Epic when the hero's future companion Enkidu shows despondency with a "drawn face."

34. Isaac Kalimi, "The Land of Moriah, Mount Moriah, and the Site of Solomon's Temple in Biblical Historiography," *HTR* 83, no. 4 (1990): 345–346.

35. Bar-Efrat, *Narrative Art*, 212–213.

36. Søren Kierkegaard, *Fear and Trembling* (Princeton: Princeton University Press, 1983), 69–70, asserts that Abraham can accept the dual concept of murdering his son while he has agreed to the religious duty of sacrificing him to God. See this interpretation in Boehm, *Binding of Isaac*, 18.

37. Landy, "Narrative Techniques and Symbolic Transactions," 13, points to an "inner necessity" on Abraham's part that corresponds to his psychological profile to be obedient.

38. Simmons, "What About Isaac?" 340.

39. Sean McEvenue, "The Elohist at Work," *ZAW* 96, no. 3 (1984): 324.

40. Note the use of the same time-based phrase in Genesis 21:14 where Abraham "rose early in the morning" to send Hagar and Ishmael on their way. The reader, aware of this previous narrative, would see a repetition of this phrase as a further link to the narrative that created Isaac as the sole heir and thus the endangerment of the heir is made that much clearer.

41. Johannnesan, "The Functions of Silence," 35, includes silence as a "lack of nonverbal efforts at communication."

42. Izydora Dambska, "Silence as an Expression and as a Value," in *Knowledge, Language and Silence* (*Poznań Studies in the Philosophy of the Sciences and the Humanities*, vol. 105; Leiden: Brill, 2016), 312, defines silence as "a conscious suspension of the process of communicating something with words."

43. Landy, "Narrative Techniques and Symbolic Transactions," 13, attempts to project the sounds and physical efforts associated with chopping wood onto Abraham's growing psychological state in

anticipation of the "murder" of the child. While I would have relished
the inclusion of a sensory aspect here, the narrative is careful to keep
sound or the kinetic aspects of physical labor out of the story until Isaac
is bound on the altar.

44. For other examples, see Exodus 15:22; Numbers 33:8; and Joshua 1:11.

45. The phrase "far away" is a geographic separator that makes it clear
that when he goes on, leaving his servants behind and out of sight, he
is about to leave mundane space and enter sacred space that is dedi-
cated to his sacrificial task. Note how after the flood in the Gilgamesh
epic, Utnapishtim and his wife are transported to Dilmun, far away
from human space and within the divine plane where they become
immortal (Matthews and Benjamin, *OTP-5*, 49–53). Utnapishtim
is also given the additional name "the Faraway" or "the remote one"
(*rêqu*) as an indicator of his inaccessibility to humankind (Tablet XI:
col. 1:1).

46. For example, Hagar's flight into the wilderness where she experiences
a theophany (Gen 16:6–14). See Thomas B. Dozeman, "The Wilderness and Salvation History in the Hagar Story," *JBL* 117, no. 1 (1998):
23–43.

47. John G. Peters, "Silence, Space, and Absence in Joseph Conrad's
African Fiction," *Texas Studies in Literature and Language* 63, no.
4 (2021): 382, points to the similar stripping away of civilization
and sound as Conrad's characters travel deeper in the emptiness of
the African forest, into "spatial silence" that is "both literal and
figurative."

48. Isabella van Elferen and Sven Raeymaekers, "Silent Dark: The Orders
of Silence" *Journal for Cultural Research* 19, no. 3 (2015): 264, in
distinguishing various forms of silence, contends that metaphorical
silence "can also represent balance" as well as "the absence of emotion,
of speech and of language."

49. Bernard P. Dauenhauer, *Silence: The Phenomenon and Its Ontological
Significance* (Bloomington: Indiana University Press, 1980), 27–29,
labels this an "interlocutor-centered discourse," one that "refers focally
to the participants' spatiotemporal situation" and to the "situation at
hand."

50. Nahum Sarna, *The JPA Torah Commentary: Genesis* (Philadelphia: JPS,
1989), 153, uses this to argue that the cultural premise here is animal,
not human sacrifice.

51. It could be compared to the way a sleepy Eli dismisses the child Samuel
when he comes to him in the middle of the night (1 Sam 3:4–8).

52. Robin Reames, "Speech in Pursuit of Silence," *Philosophy & Rhetoric* 55, no. 1 (2022): 33, notes "there are situations in which silence is required after speech has put a punctuation mark on further dialogue."

53. It is only after the altars are constructed that Abraham breaks the silence and "invoked the name of the Lord" (Gen 12:8).

54. See Isaac Kalimi, "The Land of Moriah," 345–362. This site is analogous to the unknown burial site for Moses (Deut 34:6) since both are shrouded in sacred space.

55. John Kessler, *Between Hearing and Silence: A Study in Old Testament Theology* (Waco, TX: Baylor University Press, 2021), 4, contends that in the Hebrew Bible silence is not the absence of sound or actions. Instead, it is the absence of or lack of sounds that would be expected in a particular situation.

56. Schwartz, 46, derails the argument that Abraham's very vocal argument against the divine destruction of Sodom and Gomorrah in Gen 18:25 should be paralleled with the Aqedah. He states this is not how Abraham understood human sacrifice, it "is perfectly consistent that he should object to injustice at Sodom and Gomorrah (a divine plan) but not in the Aqedah (a divine command). From his perspective, "there is no injustice in the Aqedah."

57. In most other cases sacrifices were not conducted in silence. That is especially the case for those that were performed in public where they were acknowledged/ acclaimed/ approved by the priests and the people. Israel Knohl, "Between Voice and Silence: The Relationship between Prayer and Temple Cult," *JBL* 115, no. 1 (1996): 21–23, states that silence only reigns within the temple. Outside the temple "the turbulent folk cult" is the appropriate place for the vocalized prayers, music, and songs.

58. Michal B. Dinkler, *Silent Statements: Narrative Representations of Speech and Silence in the Gospel of Luke.* (Berlin: de Gruyter, 2013), 6, points to the analysis of silence in terms of context, source, and its "interpersonal functions (silence can alienate, or silence can unify)."

59. Jef Verschueren, *What People Say They Do with Words* (Northwood, NJ: Ablex, 1985), 73, notes that the amount of silence exceeds the absence of speech. He points to silence as "golden, deathlike, tomblike, solemn, and even pregnant" but rarely a neutral condition.

60. Schwartz, 45, points out that this term is "most common in ritual, where it is ethically neutral" and thus removes the stigma of murder.

61. For an examination of this devout gesture, see Christopher G. Frechette, *Mesopotamian Ritual-prayers of "Hand-lifting" (Akkadian šuillas): An*

Investigation of Function in Light of the Idiomatic Meaning of the Rubric. (Münster: Ugarit-Verlag, 2012).

62. Bar-Efrat, *Narrative Art*, 211, points to duplication of words as a stylistic feature that in this case expresses strong emotion.

63. The summary statement in Wis 3:5–6 characterizes God's "testing" of the righteous and establishes that they are indeed "worthy of himself." Fear in this situation is an expression of trust, respect, and acknowledgment of power—all within the framework of that sentiment found in the Psalms (i.e., Ps 111:10). It is also a virtue that is intended to inspire humans to always act morally, not just when the authorities are present or punishment is imminent.

64. Ong, *Orality and Literacy*, 41, points to the practice in a "primary oral culture" of repeating stock phrases that emphasize core beliefs or values while serving as an acknowledgment of both stored memory and elements central to a story.

65. Adding to the return to normalcy, there is a reiteration of the covenant promise of offspring (Gen 22:15–18).

66. Wendy Zierler, "In Search of a Feminist Reading of the Akedah," *NASHIM: A Journal of Jewish Women's Studies and Gender* 9, no. 5765 (2005): 21, notes the crucial difference in this statement and the one in God's command to Abraham in Genesis 22:2. In this declaration of satisfaction by the deity, the appellation "whom you love" is omitted in Genesis 22:16. This is a not-so-subtle indication to the reader/audience that the relationship between father and son is fractured by this set of events.

67. Omri Boehm, "Child Sacrifice, Ethical Responsibility and the Existence of the People of Israel," *VT* 54, no. 2 (2004): 149–152, suggests that the Passover lamb in Exodus 12–13, may be a better precedent for the elimination of human sacrifice among the Israelites. Still, it does serve in the case of the Aqedah as a social precedent linked back to the ancestral narratives and may go back to a pervasive "myth of child sacrifice" in Near Eastern tradition.

68. Compare the silent lamb "led to the slaughter" in Second Isaiah's "suffering servant" song (Isa 52:7).

69. See the naming of the well in Genesis 16:14 and the renaming of Luz as Bethel in Genesis 28:19.

70. Kalimi, "The Land of Moriah, 349–350.

71. See his repeated attempts to provide himself with an heir (Lot, Eliezer, Ishmael).

72. J. Richard Middleton, *Abraham's Silence: The Binding of Isaac, the Suffering of Job, and How to Talk Back to God* (Grand Rapids, MI: Baker Academic, 2021), 197–200, traces what he calls the "arc of Abraham's discernment of God's character" and concludes that that leads to Abraham being able to break his silence and speak to God about the fate of Sodom in Genesis 18:23–32 (pp. 200–204).

73. It also raises the question of Isaac's age and whether he would have been able to return to the encampment on his own.

74. Brett, "Abraham's 'Heretical' Imperative," 173, sees this collation of place and Ishmael as the father of a "great nation" as a clue planted by the editors in the Persian period, suggesting that origin from a "mixed marriage" and Egyptian ties are "no impediment to divine blessing."

75. Zierler, "Feminist Reading of the Akedah," 20.

76. Cheryl Glenn, *Unspoken: A Rhetoric of Silence* (Carbondale: Southern Illinois University Press, 2004), 25–28.

77. It is ironic that he should be tied to the site of the pregnant Hagar's theophany after she fled from Abram's encampment (Gen 16:7–14).

78. J. Cheryl Exum, *Fragmented Women: Feminist (Sub)versions of Biblical Narratives* (Valley Forge, PA: Trinity Press International, 1993), 102.

79. Susan S. Lanser, *The Narrative Act* (Princeton: Princeton University Press, 1981), p. 241, discusses an "inquiry into absence," which questions a narrative's purpose about "what is not said, what is not shown, what points of view or narrative possibilities are not present." She also speculates (pp. 501–503) on the movement of Sarah from a silent character in Genesis 12:1, 10–20 to a very vocal character in Genesis 16 and 21, and then a silent/absent character thereafter.

80. See a summary of these efforts and Midrashic interpretations in W. Lee Humphreys, "Where's Sarah? Echoes of a Silent Voice in the 'Akedah,'" *Soundings* 81, no. 3–4 (1998): 498–501.

81. Zierler, "Feminist Reading of the Akedah," 12–14.

82. Phyllis Trible, *Texts of Terror: Literary-Feminist Readings of Biblical Narrative* (Philadelphia: Fortress, 1984), 188–189.

83. Exum, *Fragmented Women*, 102–103.

84. Booth, *Essential Wayne Booth*, 169, points to the goal of some literary offerings to provide "moral guidance." That includes "the patterning of desires and gratification that the author takes us through."

85. Humphreys, "Where's Sarah?" 492–493, describes Sarah as "direct and forceful in confronting her husband" over the threat posed by Ishmael (Gen 21:10) while noting her speech in this verse is the last

time her voice is heard in the narrative. Carey Walsh, "Under the Influence: Trust and Risk in Biblical Family Drinking," *JSOT* 25, no. 90
(2000): 22–23, points to Sarah's intoxication during the banquet (Gen
21:8–11) as a heightening factor for her resentment against Ishmael and
Hagar, "a catharsis . . . strong enough to bring on resolution" and the
demand for the expulsion of the pair.

CHAPTER THREE

1. C. Wulf, "Präsenz des Schweigens," in *Schweigen: Unterbrechung und
   Grenze der menschlichen Wirlichkeit*, eds. D. Kamper and C. Wulf
   (Berlin: Reimer, 1992), 7.
2. Kris Acheson, "Silence as Gesture: Rethinking the Nature of Commu-
   nicative Silences," *Communication Theory* 18, no. 4 (2008): 543.
3. Michal B. Dinkler, *Silent Statements: Narrative Representations of
   Speech and Silence in the Gospel of Luke* (Doctoral Dissertation, Harvard
   Divinity School, 2012), 8: https://nrs.harvard.edu/URN-3:HUL.
   INSTREPOS:37367449.
4. Occasionally, silent characters may be allowed to employ nonverbal
   forms of communication—usually gestures or facial expressions.
   Such exaggerated bodily gestures are often used to define the villain
   in wisdom literature. He is to be identified by his "crooked speech" that
   is accompanied by winking eyes, shuffling feet, and pointing fingers
   (Prov 6:12–13). See also winking eyes in Proverbs 10:10; 16:30; and
   Sirach 27:22. The expressiveness of the eyes is also communicated by the
   unfaithful wife (Sir 26:9) and the seductive eyelashes of the adulteress
   (Prov 6:25).
5. Louise Anne Nichols, *Silent Characters in Shakespeare's Plays: Text and
   Production* (PhD Dissertation; University of Toronto, 1992), 3.
6. Rebecca Wood, "Foucault, Freda Fry and the Power of Silent Characters on the Radio," in *Gender, Sex, and Gossip in Ambridge: Women
   in* The Archers, eds. Cara Courage and Nicola Headlam (Bingley,
   England: Emerald Group Publishing, 2019), 79.
7. Nichols, *Silent Characters*, 3.
8. See Wye K. Park, *Why Not Her? A Form and Literary-Critical Interpretation of the Named and Unnamed Women in the Elijah and Elisha
   Narratives* (New York: Peter Lang, 2015), 161–163, who describes the
   Israelite slave girl in 2 Kings 5:3 taking on a prophetic role, predicting
   that if the Syrian general Na'aman goes to consult Elisha about his
   leprosy, he will be healed.

9. Maria Häusl, "Women at the King's Court: Their Political, Economic, and Religious Significance in the Accounts of the Former Prophets," in Juliana Claassens, ed. *Prophecy and Gender in the Hebrew Bible* (Atlanta: SBL, 2021), 237–238.

10. A statement of regret that parallels that of the "Prodigal son" in Luke 15:11–19. Her situation, while self-imposed by her promiscuity, places her in the category of characters in a "hopeless situation" out of her control. See Wayne C. Booth, *The Rhetoric of Fiction*, 2nd ed. (Chicago: Chicago, 1983), 298.

11. Laila L. Vijayan, "Social Inquisitiveness of Prophetic Imagination and the Silenced Voice of Gomer," *Bangalore Theological Forum* 49, no. 2 (2017): 63, suggests that in silence, Gomer fulfills the metaphor's use of her as a wife, mother, and harlot.

12. Consider Jesus choosing not to answer Pilate's questions in the Synoptic accounts (Matt 27:13–14; Mark 15:3–5). Contrast this with Jesus's responses to Pilate in John 18:33–38. On this, see Norman H. Young, "The Trial of Jesus before Pilate in the Fourth Gospel: A Comparison with Mark," *EvQ* 92, no. 1 (2021): 11–13.

13. Richard Johannesen, "The Functions of Silence: A Plea for Communication Research," *Western Speech* 38, no. 1 (1974), 25, notes that "Human silence is pregnant with meaning because of the assumption that thought processes are occurring."

14. Athalya Brenner, "Rizpah [Re]membered: 2 Samuel 1–14 and Beyond," in *Performing Memory in Biblical Narrative and Beyond*, eds. Athalya Brenner and Frank H. Polak (Sheffield, England: Sheffield Phoenix Press, 2009), 208.

15. See Ahithophel's advice to Absalom to take David's ten concubines, who had been left in the palace while David is forced into exile (2 Sam 16:20–22). Note that they are a portion of the king's harem, emblematic of his power, and in this case are silent characters used as political pawns.

16. Michael A. Eischelbach, *Has Joab Foiled David? A Literary Study of the Importance of Joab's Character in Relation to David* (New York: Peter Lang, 2005), 25.

17. He may be hoping for an alliance with David to protect his territories from the Philistines.

18. Frederick H. Cryer, "David's Rise to Power and the Death of Abner: An Analysis of 1 Samuel XXVI 14–16 and Its Redaction-Critical Implications," *VT* 35, no. 4 (1985): 389.

19. Baruch Halpern, *David's Secret Demons: Messiah, Murderer, Traitor, King* (Grand Rapids, MI: Eerdmans, 2001), 306–308; James

Vanderkam, "David's Complicity in the Deaths of Abner and Eshbaal: A Historical and Redactional Study," *JBL* 99, no. 4 (1980): 521–539.

20. For a discussion of this narrative's chronological placement and the argument that it is better placed after 2 Samuel 9, see Brian N. Peterson, "The Gibeonite Revenge of 2 Samuel 21:1–14: Another Example of David's Darker Side or a Picture of a Shrewd Monarch?" *JETS* 1, no. 2 (2012): 217.

21. Compare the three-year drought and famine in 1 Kings 17:1 and 18:1.

22. See the discussion of this story's composition and literary elements in Simeon Chavel, "Compositry and Creativity in 2 Samuel 21:1–14," *JBL* 122, no. 1 (2003): 34–38. He does not see this as a form of talionic atonement but as a sacrificial offering to YHWH.

23. Brian Britt, "Death, social conflict, and the barley harvest in the Hebrew Bible," *Journal of Hebrew Scriptures* 5 (2004–2005): 6–7, argues against this being an example of human sacrifice, seeing it as a judicial act rather than a seasonal ritual designed to bring rain.

24. Kyle McCarter, *II Samuel* (New York: Doubleday, 1984), 445–446.

25. Examples of nonverbal communication appear in one of Job's reaffirmations of his innocence when he refers to God's various, nonverbal expressions of contempt for him: "gnashed his teeth at me"; "sharpens his eyes against me" (Job 16:9). Edgar Kellenberger, "Gottes Doppelrolle in Ijob 16," Bib 90, no. 2 (2009): 225–226, cites other examples of divine gnashing of teeth in Mesopotamian literature.

26. Samantha Joo, "Counter-narratives: Rizpah and the 'Comfort Women' Statue," *JSOT* 44, no. 1 (2019): 83, defines a counternarrative as a story "from the margins" that provides an alternative storyline designed "to challenge or resist the master narrative."

27. Serge Frolov and Vladimir Orel, "Rizpah on the Rock: Notes on 2 Sam. 21:1–14," *Bibbia e Oriente* 37, no. 3 (1995): 149, suggest, using Isaiah 50:2–3 as their analogous text, that she created a tent made of sackcloth that would protect the bodies of her sons from the birds and scavenging animals.

28. See Stanley D. Walters, " 'To the Rock' (2 Samuel 21:10)," *CBQ* 70, no. 3 (2008): 454–456, for the way this image is applied to the nation and to Zion "as a woman who has lost all her sons" in Isaiah 30:29 and 51:1–52:12.

29. As noted in Chavel, "Compositry and Creativity," 39–40, some scholars argue that it is Rizpah who delays their timely burial.

30. Frolov and Orel, "Rizpah on the Rock," 147.

31. See the definition for shame in Anthony I. Lipscomb, " 'They Shall be Clothed in Shame': Is Shame an Emotion in the Hebrew Bible?" *Journal of Ancient Judaism* 12, no. 2 (2021): 313–314. Shame is "a social, self-conscious emotion that arises when a person considers something about themselves to be true and bad and surmises that others in a certain social context will confirm their negative self-evaluation."

32. Robin Branch, *Jeroboam's Wife: The Enduring Contributions of the Old Testament's Least-Known Women* (Peabody, MA: Hendrickson, 2009), 52–53. Chavel, "Compositry and Creativity," 50–51, points to Rizpah's ability to "evoke a humane reaction" on David's part.

33. Joo, "Counter-narratives," 90.

34. Compare Abigail, another widow with political and economic connections whom David marries (1 Sam 25:39–42).

35. Megan L. Case, "Michal the Giver and Michal the Taker: The Systematic Misogyny of the Davidic Court," *BibInt* 31, no. 1 (2023: 54–55, sees David's "severe reaction" as necessary to quell other dissident voices and to serve as a warning to any other females in his court who wished to raise an objection to his policies and actions.

36. It serves as a prime example of the "King's Call to Justice" motif. See Victor H. Matthews, "The King's Call to Justice," *BZ* 35, no. 2 (1991): 204–216. Sara M. Koenig, "Make War Not Love: The Limits of David's Hegemonic Masculinity in 2 Samuel 10–12," BibInt 23, no. 4–5 (2015): 506–507, while discussing how the text appears to be an expression of David's hegemonic masculinity in taking any woman he wishes, notes that he is subject to the ultimate hegemonic power of YHWH and is subject to punishment when he fails to maintain self-control and breaks the rules of society.

37. There are a variety of interpretations of why David chooses to summon Bathsheba to his palace at a point in her menstrual cycle when she would be most likely to become pregnant (2 Sam 11:2). In addition, there is also the question of whether she is complicit or even the instigator in their affair. Most scholars also suggest that there are political connotations associated with their affair. See George G. Nicol, "The Alleged Rape of Bathsheba: Some Observations on Ambiguity in Biblical Narrative," *JSOT* 22, no. 73 (1997): 43–54; and Randall C. Bailey, *David in Love and War: The Pursuit of Power in 2 Samuel 10–12* (Sheffield, England: JSOT Press, 1990), 85–90.

38. David G. Firth, "(With an Occasional Appearance by Uriah's Wife): Reading and Re-Reading 2 Samuel 11," *OTE* 21, no. 2 (2008): 313.

39. McCarter, *II Samuel*, 286. Compare similar use of "feet" as a euphemism for male genitalia in Isaiah 6:2 and Ezekiel 16:25. There is some speculation about David's friendly directive here, since it could be construed as a violation of the stipulation in Deuteronomy 23:10 that soldiers on campaign were to refrain from sexual relations. Sexual activity during campaign would not be possible for soldiers within the encampment but Uriah is not at the front. See on this Bailey, *David in Love and War*, 88–90.
40. Koenig, "Make War Not Love," 510.
41. There is a comic tone here, making David look desperate in the face of Uriah's loyalty.
42. His firm stance is reminiscent of David's daughter Tamar when she tries to keep her brother Amnon from committing rape (2 Sam 13:12–16). She unsuccessfully uses the argument of "right behavior" and "wise action," saying "such a thing is not done in Israel" (2 Sam 13:12). See Victor H. Matthews and Don C. Benjamin, "Amnon and Tamar: A Matter of Honor (2 Samuel 13:1–38)," in *Crossing Boundaries and Linking Horizons: Studies in Honor of Michael C. Astour*, eds. G.D. Young, M. Chavalas, and R. E. Averbeck (coauthor, D. C. Benjamin; Bethesda, MD: CDL Press, 1997), 355–361.
43. David J. A. Clines, "David the Man: The Construction of Masculinity in the Hebrew Bible," in *Interested Parties: The Ideology of Writers and Readers of the Hebrew Bible*, ed. David J. A. Clines (JSOTSup, 205; Gender, Culture, Theory 1; Sheffield, England: Sheffield Academic, 1995), 225–226, prioritizes male bonding rather than romantic liaisons with women.
44. Jack Sasson, "The Blood of Grapes: Viticulture and Intoxication in the Hebrew Bible," in *Drinking in Ancient Societies: History and Culture of Drinks in the Ancient Near East* (Padua: Sargon, 1994), 406, argues that Uriah, despite his inebriation, would not violate the military code.
45. The alteration in the plan is an indication that Joab is shrewder than David when it comes to military matters and maintaining the morale of his men. Eischelbach, *Has Joab Foiled David*, 27, discusses the various interpretations of Joab's decision to alter David's instructions. Firth, "David and Uriah," 313–314, questions why the author expends so much time on recounting the pathway to Uriah's demise, even suggesting that the interchange with Uriah is the primary focus of the narrative and the affair with Bathsheba a secondary element.
46. Firth, "David and Uriah," 314.

47. Eschelbach, *Has Joab Foiled David*, 33–34.
48. Gregory T. K. Wong, "Ehud and Joab: Separated at Birth?" *VT* 56, no. 3 (2006): 404–405, points to Joab grasping Amasa's beard as a gesture of affection prior to a kiss of welcome.
49. See for example the unnamed wife of Manoah, the mother of Samson in Judges 13. As Adele Reinhartz, "Samson's Mother: An Unnamed Protagonist," in Athalya Brenner, ed. *Feminist Companion to* Judges (Sheffield, England: JSOT Press, 1993), 159, notes: "She has a central role and is more favorably pictured than her husband."
50. See Joseph Naveh, "Nameless People," *IEJ* 40, no. 2–3 (1990): 108–123.
    K. Paul Bednarowski, "Surprise and Suspense in Aeschylus' *Agamemnon*," *American Journal of Philology* 136, no. 2 (2015): 179, notes that "Aeschylus was known in antiquity for deriving surprise and suspense from silent characters like Achilles, Niobe, and Cassandra." He cites Judith Mossman, *Euripides: Medea* (Oxford: Oxbow, 2010), 28, who sees this narrative style as a device to "sway the audience's emotions in one direction or another."
51. Cheryl Glenn, *Unspoken: A Rhetoric of Silence* (Carbondale: Southern Illinois University Press, 2004), 11.
52. Dee Das, "Silence in Literary Fiction" (2022): https://bookriot.com/silence-in-literary-fiction/
53. See Adriane Leveen, *Memory and Tradition in the Book of Numbers* (Cambridge: Cambridge University Press, 2008), 74.
54. See Numbers 35:30 and Deuteronomy 19:15.
55. See also Deuteronomy 22:13–19, in which the husband makes a verbal charge against his wife of infidelity and her father counters that with a statement refuting the husband and then engages in a ritual displaying the physical proof of her virginity at the time of the marriage.
56. Note that this case study posits a situation in which false testimony is given by the husband and concludes with either his public humiliation or the stoning of the wife at the door of her father's house. See Bruce Wells, "Sex, Lies, and Virginal Rape: The Slandered Bride and False Accusation in Deuteronomy," *JBL* 124, no. 1 (2005): 41–72.
57. Micha Roi, "The Law of the Sotah and the Cup of Wrath: Substantive and Adjective Law in the Hebrew Bible," RB 124, no. 2 (2017): 178–179.
58. The use of "remembrance" and the repeated use of the word *zikkaron* (Num 5:15 and 5:18) reinforces the ritual role of the priest and upholds the authority of the husband to impose this test on his wife. See Leveen, *Memory and Tradition*, 74–75.

59. Jacob Milgrom, *Numbers* (Philadelphia: Jewish Publication Society, 1990), 38–39.

60. Nissim Amzallag and Shamir Yona, "The Kenite Origin of the Sotah Prescription (Numbers 5.11–31)," *JSOT* 41, no. 4 (2017): 400–403, suggests that copper salts is the active ingredient in this potion that could cause a spontaneous abortion of the fetus, demonstrating the woman's unfaithfulness and guilt.

   Ann Marie Kitz, "Effective Simile and Effective Act: Psalm 109, Numbers 5, and KUB 26," *CBQ* 69, no. 3 (2007): 452–453, discusses the taste of this potion and suggests the "bitterness" is a simile for hardship or distress.

61. Brian Britt, "Male Jealousy and the Suspected Sotah: Toward a Counter-Reading of Numbers 5:11–31," *The Bible & Critical Theory* 3, no. 1 (2007): 3–5.

62. Kitz, "Effective Simile," 453–454, calls this an example of "effective speech" designed to bring the curse, if justified, into being.

63. See William McKane, "Poison, Trial by Ordeal and the Cup of Wrath," *VT* 30, no. 4 (1980): 474–478; and Tikva Frymer-Kensky, "The Strange Case of the Suspected Sotah (Number V 11–31)," *VT* 34, no. 1 (1984): 11–26, on whether this is an example of a trial by ordeal or should be considered a test like that in Genesis 22.

64. See Victor H. Matthews, "Hospitality and Hostility in Genesis 19 and Judges 19," *BTB* 22, no. 1 (1992), 3–11. T. Desmond Alexander, "Lot's Hospitality: A Clue to His Righteousness," *JBL* 104, no. 2 (1985): 289–291, includes a discussion of the tradition of Lot's righteousness in 2 Pet 2:7–8, rabbinic literature, and the church fathers.

65. Citing other revenge stories and employing trauma theory, Kirsi Cobb, "Did Lot Get His Just Desserts? Trauma, Revenge, and Re-enactment in Genesis 19.30–38," *JSOT* 47, no. 2 (2022): 189–205, raises this possibility. In an earlier study, Kirsi Cobb, " 'Look at What They've Turned Us Into': Reading the Story of Lot's Daughters with Trauma Theory and *The Handmaid's Tale*," *Open Theology* 7 (2021): 211–212, notes that Lot's offer to the crowd abrogates his previous engagement of his daughters to men who may be in that crowd outside his door.

66. Melissa A. Jackson, "Lot's Daughters and Tamar as Tricksters and the Patriarchal Narratives as Feminist Theology," *JSOT* 26, no. 4 (2002): 29–46, styles this episode as a trickster story that is a polemic against the patriarchic system.

67. See Jonathan Grossman, " 'Associative Meanings' in the Character Evaluation of Lot's Daughters," *CBQ* 76, no. 1 (2104): 40–57, for a

discussion of whether this section of Genesis 19 is a late addition or an
integral part of the overall narrative that depicts Lot as a weak character. See also George W. Coats, "Lot: A Foil in the Abraham Saga," in
Understanding the Word: Essays in Honor of Bernhard W. Anderson, ed.
James T. Butler, et al. (JSOTSup 37; Sheffield, England: JSOT Press,
1985), 126–127.

68. Ronald S. Hendel, Chana Kronfeld, and Ilana Pardes, "Gender and
Sexuality," in *Reading Genesis: Ten Methods*, ed. Ronald S. Hendel
(Cambridge: Cambridge University Press, 2010), 71–91.

69. Michael Carden, "Genesis/*Bereshit*," in *The Queer Bible Commentary*,
eds. Deryn Guest, et al (London: SCM Press, 2006), 38–39.

70. See Sara J. Milstein, "Saul the Levite and His Concubine: The 'Allusive'
Quality of Judges 19," *VT* 66, no. 1 (2016): 95–116.

71. See Corrine L. Carvalho, "From Heroic Individual to Nameless Victim:
Women in the Social World of the Judges," in *Biblical and Humane: a
Festschrift for John F. Priest*, eds. Linda Elder, David L. Barr, and Elizbeth Struthers (Atlanta: Scholars Press, 1996), 43, n. 51. The fact that
all of the characters in Judges 19 are nameless reflects a degradation of
the social world, reflecting "a general human condition by this time in
the story line."

72. See Deuteronomy 22:20–21; Exodus 21:5–6; and the severed hands of
the statue of Dagan lying across the threshold of his temple in 1 Samuel
5:4. Victor H. Matthews, "Making Your Point: The Use of Gestures in
Ancient Israel," *BTB* 42, no. 1 (2012): 23.

73. See Cynthia Miller, "Silence as a Response in Biblical Hebrew Narrative: Strategies of Speakers and Narrators," *JNSL* 32, no. 1 (2006): 35.

74. David Adamo, "The Unheard Voices in the Hebrew Bible: The Nameless and Silent Wife of Jeroboam (1 Kgs 14:1–18)," *OTE* 33, no. 3
(2020): 402, quotes the Egyptian sage Ptah-hotep with the admonition:
"silence is a virtue." He notes that Egyptian wisdom literature advises
appropriate reactions under three specific situations: (1) an equal opponent (2) a greater opponent, and (3) an inferior opponent. In each case,
silence, the refusal to speak, is the best reaction.

75. Shimon Bar-Efrat, *Narrative Art in the Bible* (Sheffield, England: Almond
Press, 1989), 72–73, defines this as a speech "intended to impel someone
to action," and when the person who receives the order is of a lower status
than the speaker, it generally "does not develop into a dialogue."

76. Cynthia Miller, "Silence as a Response," 35, adds that "the lack of a
response following a command is particularly stark when the command
ends a pericope" as it does in 1 Kgs 11:26–40.

77. Stuart Lasine, "Reading Jeroboam's Intentions: Intertextuality, Rhetoric, and History in 1 Kings 12," in *Reading Between Texts: Intertextuality and the Hebrew Bible*, ed. Dana N. Fewell (Louisville: Westminster/John Knox, 1992), 140–141. It would be possible to extend this assertion to the scene with his wife. His decision to send her to Ahijah is another example of "self-will" that stands in the way of good judgment.

78. Keith Bodner, *Jeroboam's Royal Drama* (New York: Oxford, 2012), 122.

79. Bodner, *Jeroboam's Royal Drama*, 123–124, speculates on the lack of any mention of Jeroboam's harem in the narrative. It is likely that this was an intentional narrative gap employed by the Deuteronomist to demonstrate the difference between Jeroboam and the large number of wives in the harem of David and Solomon.

80. Robin G. Branch, "The Wife of Jeroboam, 1 Kings 14:1–18: The Incredible, Riveting, History-Changing Significance of an Unnamed, Overlooked, Ignored, Obscure, Obedient Woman," *OTE* 17, no. 2 (2004): 159, sees her unnamed status as a lack of respect by the narrator. She also notes Jeroboam's lack of empathy, grief, or "shared grief" at the state of his son.

    Branch, "The Wife of Jeroboam," 159, refers to the narrator as an "omnipresent but not omniscient narrator," "eavesdropping" on the scene between Jeroboam and his wife.

81. Branch, "The Wife of Jeroboam," 160, suggests that this is an effort by Jeroboam to manipulate an aged, blind prophet.

    Consider the example of the high-ranking general Hazael consulting Elisha about the health of his king Ben-hadad (2 Kgs 8:7–15). There may also be a narrative parallel with Elisha sending his servant Gehazi to check on the Shunammite woman's son (2 Kgs 4:29–31).

82. Ahouva Shulman, "Imperative and Second Person Indicative Forms in Biblical Hebrew Prose," *Hebrew Studies* 42 (2001): 274, notes that "utterances in which urgency is expressed are naturally more subjective and emotional.... [intended to convey] "his will that the addressee act immediately." Expanding on this (p. 276), is the statement that imperatives are used by speakers who are superior and who expect their command to be carried out immediately. See David's command to Joab in 2 Sam 11:6.

    Robert Alter, *The Art of Biblical Narrative* (New York: Basic Books, 1981), 80. Note that Ahijah uses the same imperative command to Jeroboam's wife in 1 Kings 14:7 and 12.

83. Adamo, "The Unheard Voices in the Hebrew Bible," 403, suggests that Jeroboam is a manipulative character, and his wife's silence is characteristic of the "theme of obedience" in the Jeroboam cycle.

84. Esther Fuchs, "The Literary Characterization of Mothers and the Sexual Politics in the Hebrew Bible," in *Women in the Hebrew Bible: A Reader*, ed. Alice Bach (New York: Routledge, 1999), 136–137, provides an indication of a mother's concern and willingness to do anything to help her child.

85. Branch, "The Wife of Jeroboam," 160, speculates without further proof that the wife's silence is based on her being a "victim of verbal abuse" and her silence is an indication of her scorn for her husband. It may be a form of retaliation or simply an indication of her hopelessness in trying to discuss anything with him. Adamo, "The Unheard Voices in the Hebrew Bible," 404, says the wife's silence may be an attempt to "retaliate" against him and perhaps a demonstration of her indignation. Certainly, she must have been sorrowful after hearing the prophet's words and the condemnation of her son. But it is possible that her continued silence could be viewed as a sign of her compassion and courage as she did what her husband refused to do himself.

86. Keith Bodner. *Jeroboam's Royal Drama*, 126–127.

87. See Branch, "The Wife of Jeroboam," 161.

88. Adamo, "The Unheard Voices in the Hebrew Bible," 395, sees her silence as evidence of "her obedience, humility, peace, and self-control." On p. 398, he raises the question of reaction: surprise, tears, speechlessness based on the prophetic word.

89. Ronald A. Geobey, "The Jeroboam Story in the (Re)Formulation of Israelite Identity: Evaluating the Literary-Ideological Purposes of 1 Kings 11–14," *Journal of Hebrew Studies* 16, no. 2 (2016): 15, points to her returning to Tirzah as a narrative device that helps to establish that Jeroboam's capital is here rather than Shechem and is based on Ahijah's second prophecy.

90. Acheson, "Silence as Gesture," 538–539, discusses nonverbal forms of communication, including kinetic behaviors and vocalizations (moans, squeals, signs), as accompanying speech or replacing it with these variations on a silent (unspoken) response.

91. Branch, "The Wife of Jeroboam," 164. See Adele Reinhartz, "Anonymous Women and the Collapse of the Monarchy: A Study in the Narrative Technique," in *A Feminist Companion to Samuel and Kings*, ed. Athalya Brenner (Sheffield, England: Sheffield, 1994), 43–65. Adamo, "The Unheard Voices in the Hebrew Bible," 394, notes that there are 722 nameless persons in the OT and states that "namelessness effaces personal identity." Athalya Brenner, "Introduction," in *Feminist Companion to Judges*, ed. Athalya Brenner (Sheffield, England: JSOT

Press, 1993), 13, states that namelessness "symbolizes the suppression of women in the OT."

92. Branch, "The Wife of Jeroboam," 165.

93. See the restrictions placed on speech in Esth 5:1–3. The custom was that no one could speak to the king of Persia without being given permission through the gesture of holding out "the golden scepter" in the king's hand. See Robert L. Scott, "Dialectical Tensions of Speaking and Silence," *Quarterly Journal of Speech* 79, no. 1 (1993): 10, who notes that "the very structure of privilege will generate silences."

CHAPTER FOUR

1. Graham Turner, *The Power of Silence: The Riches That Lie Within* (New York: Bloomsbury, 2012), 91–92, describes such a moment when characters in a play walk forward and stand silently, pulling together the pathos that had come before in conversation and now drawing the audience into silent reflection.

2. George Prochnik, *In Pursuit of Silence: Listening for Meaning in a World of Noise* (New York: Doubleday, 2010), 14–20.

3. Bernard P. Dauenhauer, *Silence: The Phenomenon and Its Ontological Significance* (Bloomington, IN: Indiana University Press, 1980), 16–17.

4. See Numbers 10:5–6 for the signal for the tribal encampments to depart. Exod 19:13–19, Josh 6:5, and Zeph 1:16 use the blast and different levels of sounds as signals.

5. Werner Enninger, "Focus on Silence Across Cultures," *Intercultural Communication* Studies 1, no. 1 (1991): 4.

6. Kris Acheson, "Silence as Gesture: Rethinking the Nature of Communicative Silence," *Communication Theory* 18, no. 4 (2008): 539.

7. Robert L. Scott, "Dialectical Tensions of Speaking and Silence," *Quarterly Journal of Speech* 79, no. 1 (1993): 7.

8. See the shocked reaction of the person without a wedding garment in Matthew 22:12. See David C. Sim, "The Man Without the Wedding Garment (Matthew 22:11–13)," *HeyJ* 31, no. 2 (1990): 176, for a discussion of this "man" serving as a composite figure, representing both the unrighteous invitees and the Jewish hierarchy who oppose the Matthean community.

9. Daniel's physical and mental reactions to his visions are also chronicled in Daniel 7:29 and 8:27. See Tim Meadowcroft, "Who are the Princes of Persia and Greece (Daniel 10)? Pointers Towards the Danielic Vision of Earth and Heaven," *JSOT* 29, no. 1 (2004): 106.

10. Jack Bilmes, "Constituting Silence: Life in the World of Total Meaning," *Semiotica* 98, no. 1–2 (1994): 78, notes that silent astonishment results from an action like this as a violation of expected social rules or protocols.

11. Joseph Blenkinsopp, *Isaiah 40–55* (New York: Doubleday, 2002), 349, ties this passage to Isaiah 49:7 in which the kings prostrate themselves before the Servant.

12. Sonja Noll, *The Semantics of Silence in Biblical Hebrew* (London: Brill, 2020), 161–162.

13. Erhard S. Gerstenberger, *Leviticus* (Louisville: Westminster/John Knox, 1996), 117, frames this scene as depicting the elimination of a rival priestly group and discusses the meaning of the "illegitimate fire" as the use of an improper mixture or coals not taken from the great altar (see Lev 16:12).

14. Compare YHWH's command that Jeremiah "not enter the house of mourning, or go to lament, or bemoan" his dead (Jer 16:5).

15. David A. Bosworth, "Daughter Zion and Weeping in Lamentations 1–2," *JSOT* 38, no. 2 (2013): 217–237.

16. F. W. Dobbs-Allsopp, "R(az/ais)ing Zion in Lamentations 2," in *David and Zion: Biblical Studies in Honor of J. J. M. Roberts*, eds. Bernard Batto and Kathryn L. Roberts (Winona Lake, IN: Eisenbrauns, 2004), 40.

17. See Wabayanga R. Kuloba, "Athaliah of Judah (2 Kings 11): A Political Anomaly or an Ideological Victim?" in *Looking Through a Glass Bible: Postdisciplinary Biblical Interpretations from the Glasgow School*, eds. A. K. M. Adam and Samuel Tongue (Leiden: Brill, 2014), 139–152.

18. Patricia Dutcher-Walls, *Narrative Art, Political Rhetoric: The Case of Athaliah and Joash* (Sheffield, England: Sheffield Academic Press, 1996), 48 and 85, sees the people in this story as a "collective character" and their quiet as a narrative form of punctuation on Athaliah's story.

19. Of course, no city is ever totally silent. In this case the political implications of her death and the elevation of her son Jehoash to the throne marked a new day and fresh hope for the future.

20. The frustration that has silenced Job's "tribunal" then comes out in the rather rude and disrespectful way that Elihu addresses him after older heads have had their opportunity. Stuart J. Foster, " 'Hey, you! Job! Listen up.' Elihu's Use of Job's Name and Its Implications for Translation," *OTE* 29, no. 3 (2016): 455–468.

21. George Savran, "The Time of Her Life: Ruth and Naomi," *Nashim* 30, no. 5777 (2016): 7–23. He asserts that Ruth sets aside the arguments

that Naomi makes regarding the need for a husband and children and instead espouses the bond between women that transcends the socio-utilitarian views of Naomi.

22. Saul Olyan, *Biblical Mourning: Ritual and Social Dimensions* (Oxford: Oxford, 2004), 14–17, describes the "incompatibility and opposition of mourning and rejoicing."

23. See Olyan, *Biblical Mourning*, 65–68, for the use of petitionary mourning in Joel 1–2. He also points to tearing garments, fasting, and weeping as forms of "self-abasement" demonstrating a humbling posture in examining Josiah's behavior in 2 Kgs 22:11–20 (p. 78).

24. Diana Lipton, "Early Mourning? Petitionary Versus Posthumous Ritual in Ezekiel XXIV," *VT* 56, no. 2 (2006): 186.

25. Yisca Zimran, " 'Look, the King Is Weeping and Mourning!': Expressions of Mourning in the David Narratives and Their Interpretative Contribution," *JSOT* 41, no. 4 (2018): 508–509, sees David's failure to engage in mourning practices after the death of the child as David's acceptance of the death and his failure to influence YHWH.

26. Stephen L. Cook, "The Speechless Suppression of Grief in Ezekiel 24:15–27: The Death of Ezekiel's Wife and the Prophet's Abnormal Response," in *Thus Says the Lord: Essays on the Former and Latter Prophets in Honor of Robert R. Wilson*, eds. John J. Ahn and Stephen L. Cook (New York: T & T Clark, 2009), 222–223.

27. Their hardly audible whimper is comparable to Aaron's "silence" in Leviticus 10:3 and the silent stance of the "elders of daughter Zion" in Lamentations 2:10. See Baruch A. Levine, "Silence, Sound, and the Phenomenology of Mourning in Biblical Israel," *JANES* 22 (1993): 89–92.

28. Cook, "Speechless Suppression," 226–229, notes that this is not directly tied to Ezekiel's role as a priest who would be expected to separate himself from contact with the dead or with death rituals.

29. Olyan, *Biblical Mourning*, 17–18.

30. For examples of this reversal see Isaiah 61:1–3 and Jeremiah 31:13.

31. For a fuller study of this prophetic genre, see the essays in Andrew Mein, Else K. Holt, and Hyn Chui Paul Kim, eds. *Concerning the Nations: Essays on the Oracles Against the Nations in Isaiah, Jeremiah, and Ezekiel* (London: Bloomsbury T & T Clark, 2015).

32. Similar mourning practices are listed in Ezekiel 27:30–32 in the "lamentation over Tyre" and its destruction.

33. Compare Job's mourning ritual in which he tears his robe, shaves his head, and falls to the ground to worship YHWH. He then voices a

prayer blessing YHWH's name despite the loss of his children (Job 1:20–21). Richard W. Medina, "Job's Entrée into a Ritual of Mourning as Seen in the Opening Prose of the Book of Job," *Die Welt des Orients* 38 (2008): 199, considers Job's actions to be a signal of "a social transition in his life."

34. Robert P. Carroll, *Jeremiah* (Philadelphia: Westminster, 1986), 777. John B. Geyer, *Mythology and Lament: Studies in the Oracles about the Nations* (Burlington, VT: Ashgate Publishing, 2004), identifies rising of the waters (Jer 47:2) as an explicit mythological reference to creation.

35. John Goldingay, "What Happens to Ms Babylon in Isaiah 47, Why, and Who Says So," *TynBul* 47, no. 2 (1996): 217–228.

36. John E. Hartley, *Leviticus* (Dallas, TX: Word Books, 1992), 315.

37. See Noll, *Semantics of Silence*, 23.

38. Raanan Eichler, "A Sin is Borne: Clearing up the Law of Women's Vows (Number 30)," *VT* 71, no. 3 (2021): 317–328.

39. Jacob Milgrom, *Numbers* (Philadelphia: Jewish Publication Society, 1990), 250–252. Note that a man who makes this type of votive pledge is obligated to present it (Deut 12:26).

40. Joseph Fleishman, "Legal Innovation in Deuteronomy XXI 18–20," *VT* 53, no. 3 (2003): 311–327, suggests that this legal statement attempts to limit capital punishment by its progressive set of charges against the son that must be met before capital punishment is applied.

41. See F. Rachel Magdalene, "Trying the Crime of Abuse of Royal Authority in the Divine Courtroom and the Incident of Naboth's Vineyard," in *The Divine Courtroom in Comparative Perspective*, eds. Art Mermeistein and Shalom E. Hotz (Leiden: Brill, 2015), 186–191, for an evaluation of the divine courtroom as the last court of appeal when kings abuse their power.

42. Note the use of the phrase "blot out their name" in Deuteronomy 7:24 in reference to the defeat of enemy kings and in Deuteronomy 12:3 for the gods of the nations, and in Deuteronomy 29:19–20 for Israelites who continue to practice idolatry. The legal premise in the law of levirate obligation (Deut 25:5–10) is to prevent a man without an heir from having his name blotted out of Israel.

43. L. Daniel Hawk, *Joshua* (Collegeville, MN: Liturgical Press, 2000), 154–156, ties the battle of Gibeon, with its miraculous elements, divine intervention, and utter defeat of the five kings together, pointing out the use of puns in the Hebrew.

44. Robert L. Scott, "Dialectical Tensions of Speaking and Silence," *Quarterly Journal of Speech* 79, no. 1 (1993): 15.

45. Similar language occurs in Habakkuk 2:20 of an awakening YHWH in his holy temple. Noll, *Semantics of Silence*, 242, contrasts the silence of idols with the God who can speak.

46. Jakob Wöhrle, " 'No Future for the Proud Exultant Ones': The Exilic Book of the Four Prophets (Hos., Am., Mic., Zeph.) as a Concept Opposed to the Deuteronomistic History," *VT* 58, no. 4–5 (2008): 618–619. See similar warnings in Micah 5:9 and Zeph 3:11.

47. Yvonne Sherwood, "Of Fruit and Corpses and Wordplay Visions: Picturing Amos 8.1–3," *JSOT* 25, no. 92 (2001): 9–10, draws out the analogy of mounting corpses and a bowl of decaying summer fruit as the visuals, shocking the people to stop and listen. See also William J. Urbrock, "The Book of Amos: The Sounds and the Silences," *CurTM* 23, no. 4 (1996): 257, n. 17, for the caution in Amos 6:9–10 as disaster and death mount, requiring the people to "hush" and not speak the name of God.

48. Compare God's command to Moses, "Never speak to me of this matter again!" (Deut 3:26) when Moses asked to cross into the Promised Land. Absalom's command to his sister Tamar, "Be quiet for now" (2 Sam 13:20), and Hezekiah's command to the besieged people of Jerusalem to be "silent and answer him (the Rabshakeh) not a word" (2 Kgs 18:36) also fall into this silencing category. There is a failed effort to silence a blind man when he shouts for Jesus's attention (Luke 18:37–39).

49. See Jordan W. Jones, "An Embodiment of Silence: The Hand-on-Mouth Gesture in the Hebrew Bible and Ancient Near East," in *The Body: Lived, Cultured, Adorned: Essays on Dress and the Body and Ancient Near East in Honor of Nili S. Fox*, eds. Angela R. Erisman, et al (Cincinnati: HUC Press, 2022), 50–55. Other examples of the gesture appear in Mic 7:16; Prov 30:32; Job 21:5; 29:9; 40:4.

50. Robert P. Clair, *Organizing Silence* (Albany, NY: University of New York Press, 1998), 21.

51. See Elizabeth Noelle-Neumann, *The Spiral of Silence: Public Opinion— Our Social Skin* (Chicago: University of Chicago Press, 1984), 8–37, for empirical measurement tools to test this shift.

52. McBride, S. Dean, "Jeremiah and the Levitical Priests of Anathoth," in *Thus Says the Lord: Essays on the Former and Latter Prophets in Honor of Robert R. Wilson*, eds. John J. Ahn and Stephen L. Cook (New York: T&T Clark, 2009), 189–190, includes this passage as part of a collection of indictments against Jeremiah's opponents.

53. Samuel Hildebrandt, "When Words Become Too Violent: Silence as a Form of Nonviolent Resistance in the Book of Jeremiah," *BibInt* 29, no. 2 (2012): 188.

54. Benjamin Foreman, "Strike the Tongue: Silencing the Prophet in Jeremiah 18:18b," *VT* 59, no. 4 (2009): 653–657.

55. Yariv Tsfati and Shira Dvir-Gvirsman, "Silencing Fellow Citizens: Conceptualization, Measurement, and Validation of a Scale for Measuring the Belief in the Importance of Actively Silencing Others," *International Journal of Public Opinion Research* 30, no. 3 (2018): 392.

56. Else K. Holt, "Word of Jeremiah—Word of God: Structures of Authority in the Book of Jeremiah," in *Uprooting and Planting: Essays on Jeremiah for Leslie Allen*, ed. John Goldingay (New York: T & T Clark, 2007), 175.

57. Alice Deken, "Does Prophecy Cause History? Jeremiah 36: A Scroll Ablaze," *OTE* 30, no. 3 (2017): 631, points to the symbolism of a scroll on fire and a burning Jerusalem as well as Jehoiakim's rejection of Jeremiah's message. William A. Holladay, *Jeremiah 2* (Minneapolis: Fortress, 1989), 260, contrasts the reactions of the king's advisers in Jeremiah 36:1–19 and those in the king's audience chamber (Jer 36:24). The difference is based on private vs. public reading of the scroll and the willingness of the second group of advisers to parrot the response of the king.

58. Noelle-Neumann, *Spiral of Silence*, 6–7, 37–41; Gina M. Masullo and Marley Duchovnay, "Extending the Spiral of Silence: Theorizing a Typology of Political Self-Silencing," *Communication Studies* 73, no. 5–6 (2022): 607–622.

59. J. Todd Hibbard, "True and False Prophecy: Jeremiah's Revision of Deuteronomy," *JSOT* 35, no. 3 (2011): 342–349.

60. Hildebrandt, "When Words Become Too Violent," 201–202, sees Jeremiah's actions as a deliberate strategy, employing silence to shatter the false hope raised by Hananiah.

61. Jacob Shamir, "Speaking Up and Silencing Out in Face of a Changing Climate of Opinion," *Journalism & Mass Communication Quarterly* 74, no. 3 (1997): 602–603.

62. For a fuller discussion, see Victor H. Matthews, "The Many Forms and Foundations of Power and Authority in the Hebrew Bible," in *T & T Clark Handbook of Anthropology and the Hebrew Bible*, ed. Emanuel Pfoh (London: T & T Clark, 2023), 189–204.

63. E. Michael Bannester, "Sociodynamics: An Integrative Theorem of Power, Authority, Interfluence and Love," *American Sociological Review* 34, no. 3 (1969): 375, calls this "sociomotive power."

64. Heinrich Popitz, *Phenomena of Power: Authority, Domination, and Violence* (New York: Columbia University Press, 2017), 5.

65. Jesus demonstrates his authority by commanding the "unclean spirit" to "be silent!" (Mark 1:25; Luke 4:35).

66. Cheryl Glenn, *Unspoken: A Rhetoric of Silence* (Carbondale: Southern Illinois University Press, 2004), 10–11, notes that there are persons who are silenced because their words have no influence. In other instances, it is the situation that requires silence such as a courtroom or during a funeral.

67. Michal Ephratt, *Silence as Language: Verbal Silence as a Means of Expression* (Cambridge: Cambridge, 2022), 24, points to the use of silencing to control subordinates or protesters.

68. Michael Freeden, "Silence in Political Theory: A Conceptual Predicament," *Journal of Political Ideologies* 20, no. 1 (2015): 3.

69. Marjo Korpel and Johannes de Moor. *The Silent God* (Leiden: Brill, 2011), 101, refer to this as the "silence of incapacity."

70. Gene Rice, "Elijah's Requirement for Prophetic Leadership (2 Kings 2:1–18)," *Journal of Religious Thought* 59, no. 1 (2006): 4, sees the existence of these companies of prophets at Gilgal, Bethel, and Jericho as a "new development in the prophetic movement that serves to "acknowledge the leadership and authority" of Elijah and then Elisha.

71. Barry Brummett, "Towards a Theory of Silence as a Political Strategy," *The Quarterly Journal of Speech* 66, no. 3 (1980): 290.

72. Mark A. O'Brien, "The Portrayal of Prophets in 2 Kings 2," *Australian Biblical Review* 46 (1998): 3–5. He adds that the "company of prophets" functions as a "collective character" rather than a group of individuals.

73. Omer Sergi, "Saul, David, and the Formation of the Israelite Monarchy," in *Saul, Benjamin, and the Emergence of Monarchy in Israel,* eds. Joachim J. Krause, Omer Sergi, and Kristin Weingart (Atlanta: SBL, 2020), 77, styles David's military exploits with the Philistines as the basis for David's eventual rise to the throne and evidence of Saul's failure as a leader.

74. David Jobling, "Saul's Fall and Jonathan's Rise: Tradition and Redaction in 1 Sam 14:1–46," *JBL* 95, no. 3 (1976): 369–371, characterizes Saul as jealous of his son's successes and fears he has been replaced by him "as the one through whom YHWH acts on Israel's behalf."

75. This casting of lots to determine a culprit is comparable to Joshua 7:10–21 when Achan steals from the *herem*-dedicated goods at Jericho.

76. Marsha C. White, "Saul and Jonathan in 1 Samuel 1 and 14," in *Saul in Story and Tradition*, ed. Carl S. Ehrlich (Berlin: Mohr Siebeck, 2006), 128–135, argues that Saul's oath is a sign of his piety rather than desperation. His story is then to be compared to the Aqedah, in which a father is spared taking his son's life.

77. Scott, "Dialectical Tensions of Speaking and Silence," 11, notes that "attentive silence to authority . . . marks authority as authority."

78. Noll, *Semantics of Silence,* 236. Gören Eidevall, "Sounds of Silence in Biblical Hebrew: A Lexical Study," *VT* 62, no. 2 (2012): 165, points to the use of the *hiphil* form of the word *hāšā* to command silence.

79. Compare the similar use of the phrase *va-yahas*, "hush," in Judges 3:19 and Zechariah 2:13.

80. Jaeyoung Jeon, "The Scout Narrative (Numbers 13) as a Territorial Claim in the Persian Period," *JBL* 139, no. 2 (2020): 263, notes the consensus that Caleb's abrupt intrusion into the narrative is secondary to the non-priestly story.

81. Paul receives respect and a silenced audience when he speaks to them in the vernacular language of Aramaic while at the same time preventing the Roman tribune from understanding his words (Acts 21:40–22:2).

82. Noll, *Semantics of Silence,* 236–237.

83. Steven R. Goldzwig, "Demagoguery, Democratic Dissent, and 'Re-Visioning' Democracy," *Rhetoric & Public Affairs* 9, no. 3 (2006): 474–475, suggests that the speaker's rhetoric combines with the audience's willingness to translate the body of the speech into their everyday understanding of the world.

84. Seth Sanders, "Absalom's Audience (2 Samuel 15–19)," *JBL* 138, no. 3 (2019): 514.

85. Song-Mi Suzie Park, "The Frustration of Wisdom: Wisdom, Counsel, and Divine Will in 2 Samuel 17:1–23," *JBL* 128, no. 3 (2009): 455–458, posits that Hushai's advice is taken over that of Ahithophel's because it is couched in a "wise" form, sounding wiser than it was.

86. Noll, *Semantics of Silence in Biblical Hebrew,* 31–33, notes that the *hiphil* form of the Hebrew word *hārēš* indicates "lack of action" by the people.

87. Jeffrey H. Tigay, *Deuteronomy* (Philadelphia: Jewish Publication Society, 1996), 251 and 394, n. 28, notes that *hasket* is a hapax legomenon, a word that only appears once and obtains its meaning from Akkadian and Arabic cognates.

88. Moses obtains a military victory over the Amalekites by silently holding up his staff, with a little assistance from Aaron and Hur (Exod 17:8–13). David wins a battle over the Philistines while silently waiting to hear "the sound of marching in the balsam trees" (2 Sam 5:23–24).

89. Michal Ephratt, "The Functions of Silence," 1913–1918, refers to this as an "eloquent silence" and describes it as an active form of communication.

90. See Rebekah Haigh, "Silencing the Land: Joshua as a Military Ritualist," *BibInt* 31, no. 2 (2023): 159–164, 168–169, who terms this ritual act as a form of sympathetic magic with the silent march serving as a performative force to create cessation.

91. See Gordon C. I. Wong, "Faith in the Present Form of Isaiah VII 1–17," *VT* 51, no. 4 (2001): 535–547, for a careful analysis of the role of faith in this narrative and the possible contribution of political alliances as historical background.

92. Victor H. Matthews, "Messengers and the Transmission of Information in the Mari Kingdom," in *Go to the Land I Will Show You: Studies in Honor of Dwight W. Young*, Victor H. Matthews and Joseph Coleson, eds. (Winona Lake, IN: Eisenbrauns Publishers, 1996), 267–274, discusses the role of the messenger as part of diplomatic activity as well as the possibility that they did function as spies (p. 273). See the Instructions of Ptah-hotep (7:3–5): "if you become a trusted messenger . . . speak your message to the letter" (Matthews and Benjamin, *OTP*-5, 343).

93. Saul M. Olyan, "Honor, Shame, and Covenant Relations in Ancient Israel and Its Environment," *JBL* 115, no. 2 (1996): 204–208.

94. T. M. Lemos, "Shame and Mutilation of Enemies in the Hebrew Bible," *JBL* 125, no. 2 (2006): 232–234, discusses other examples of shaming that result in symbolic castration.

95. Samuel A. Meier, *The Messenger in the Ancient Semitic World* (HSM 45; Atlanta: Scholars Press, 1988), 137–140.

96. Olyan, "Honor, Shame, and Covenant Relations," 213, n. 38.

97. Scott, "Dialectical Tensions," 15, terms the unspeakable a form of verbal taboo.

98. Compare the demands of the Aramean king Ben-Hadad when he laid siege to Samaria (1 Kgs 20:1–6).

99. Dominic Rudman, "Is the Rabshakeh also Among the Prophets? A Rhetorical Study of 2 Kings XVIII 17–35," *VT* 50, no. 1 (2000): 101–102.

100. Cynthia Miller, "Silence as a Response in Biblical Hebrew Narrative: Strategies of Speakers and Narrators," *JNSL* 32, no. 1 (2006): 33–34.

101. Noll, *Semantics of* Silence, 24. Rudman, "Is the Rabshakeh Also Among the Prophets?" 109, frames the speech as appropriate since it simply calls on the people of Jerusalem to recognize who (in this case Sennacherib) is doing the will of YHWH.

102. Ehud Ben Zvi, "Who Wrote the Speech of Rabshakeh and When?" *JBL* 109, no. 1 (1990): 86–88.

103. Although the siege was listed, Sennacherib had humiliated Hezekiah, and the Assyrian Annals make an accounting of the huge ransom paid. See Matthews and Benjamin, *OTP-5*, 224–225.

104. This label applies to two groups. First are those who are socially liminal: the female prisoner of war (Deut 21:10–14) or the debt slave who consents to perpetual servitude by having his ear pierced at the door of his master (Deut 15:16–17). They are transitioning by entering a permanent covenant with a household. Second are outsiders, who are known to a household and have established economic or political covenants with the household (Deut 16:11). See Don C. Benjamin, *The Social World of Deuteronomy: A New Feminist Commentary* (Cambridge: James Clarke & Co., 2017), 115–116, 134–135; and Mark Glanville, 'The *Gēr* (Stranger) in Deuteronomy: Family for the Displace,' *JBL* 137, no. 3 (2018): 603.

105. Hildebrandt, "When Words Become Too Violent," 204, considers Absalom's command to be "complicity in violent acts." More likely, it is a political calculation and evidence that Absalom is not yet strong enough to try to erase this shaming of his household.

106. Victor H. Matthews and Don C. Benjamin, "Amnon and Tamar: a Matter of Honor (2 Sam 13:1–38)," in *Crossing Boundaries and Linking Horizons: Studies in Honor of Michael C. Astour*, eds. Gordon D. Young, Mark Chavalas, and Richard E. Averbeck (Bethesda, MD: CDL Press, 1997), 359–361.

107. Ryan S. Higgins, "He Would Not Hear Her Voice: From Skilled Speech to Silence in 2 Samuel 13:1–22," *Journal of Feminist Studies in Religion* 36, no. 2 (2020): 33.

108. Dana L. Cloud, "The Null Persona: Race and the Rhetoric of Silence in the Uprising of '34," *Rhetoric & Public Affairs* 2, no. 2 (1999): 179.

109. Scott, "Dialectical Tensions," 5, notes that in times when the people may become disorderly in pursuing their own needs blindly, then circumstances make it necessary to remain silent, not out of respect

but as a means of self-preservation. That seems to be the case in Paul's admonition to the Corinthian Christians that if there is no one available to interpret a "tongue," then that person should remain "silent in church and speak to themselves and to God" (1 Cor 14:28).

110. Hildebrandt, "When Words Become Too Violent," 197–198, refers to this as a strategy of disengagement. The author of 1 Peter 2:15 goes further by saying it is a good thing to "silence the ignorant talk of foolish men."

111. Urbrock, "The Book of Amos," 252, suggests this refers to those wise enough to listen to prophecy at a moment when judgment is near.

112. Noll, *Semantics of Silence*, 48.

113. A. Graeme Auld, *I & II Samuel: A Commentary* (Louisville, KY: Westminster/John Knox, 2011), 117.

114. P. Kyle McCarter, *1 Samuel* (New York: Doubleday, 1980), 195–196.

115. Compare the powers invested in Jeremiah at the time of his call as a prophet: "to pluck up and to pull down, to destroy and to overthrow, to build and to plant" (Jer 1:10).

116. David Wolfers, "Reflections on Job xii," *VT* 44, no. 3 (1994): 405, uses this passage to argue that the context of Job is the period in which the Assyrians ravage Israel and Judah in the 8th century BCE.

117. Marc Z. Brettler, "(Divine) Silence is Golden: A New Reading of the Prologue of Job," in *Interested Readers: Essays on the Hebrew Bible in Honor of David J. A. Clines*, eds. James K. Aitken, Jeremy M.S. Clines, and Christi M. Maier (Atlanta: SBL, 2013), 19–26.

118. See Linda Day, "Rhetoric and Domestic Violence in Ezekiel 16," *BibInt* 8, no. 3 (2000): 215–216, sees calming as one of the stages of a domestic batterer.

119. See Noll, *Semantics of Silence*, 175–177.

120. Matthews and Benjamin, *OTP-5*, 343 and 364.

121. Compare James 1:19 for the rule to "be quick to listen, slow to speak."

122. See Jurgen Ebach, "Silence in the Bible: A Short Introduction and Seven Miniatures," *Concilium* 5 (2012): 106, for a discussion of when it is appropriate to speak or keep silent.

CHAPTER FIVE

1. John Kessler, *Between Hearing and Silence: A Study of Old Testament Theology* (Waco, TX: Baylor, 2021), 4.

2. Isabella van Elferen and Sven Raeymaekers, "Silent Dark: The Orders of Silence," *Journal for Cultural Research* 19, no. 3 (2015): 262.

3. Jef Verschueren, *What People Say They Do with Words* (Northwood, NJ: Ablex, 1985), 73.
4. Marjo Korpel and Johannes de Moor, *The Silent God* (Leiden: Brill, 2011), 55.
5. See the silencing of the sea in Psalms 19:3; 65:7, 89:9 and 107:29 (compare Mark 4:25–41). These events stand in contrast with those times when God's voice is the basis for creation (Gen 1; Ps 33:6, 9).
6. There is a similar sequence in the Ugaritic Epic of Kirta with a pause of satisfaction after the birth of his sons and daughters over the course of seven years. See Michael D. Coogan and Mark S. Smith, *Stories from Ancient Canaan*, 2nd ed. (Louisville, KY: Westminster/John Knox, 2012), 83–84.
7. Samuel Terrien, *The Elusive Presence: The Heart of Biblical Theology* (San Francisco: Harper & Row, 1983), 321.
8. Kris Acheson, "Silence as Gesture: Rethinking the Nature of Communicative Silences," *Communication Theory* 18, no. 4 (2008): 535–555.
9. See Cynthia Miller, "Silence as a Response in Biblical Hebrew Narrative: Strategies of Speakers and Narrators," *JNSL* 32, no. 1 (2006): 30, for a discussion of 1 Sam 14:37. For her, "silence by the deity is uniformly represented as the absence of a response."
10. Nancy C. Lee, *Lyrics of Lament: From Tragedy to Transformation* (Minneapolis: Fortress, 2010), 29–30, points to an "energizing" of the Israelites by the belief in a deity willing to act on their behalf.
11. Joel Burnett, "Divine Silence or Divine Absence? Converging Metaphors in Family Religion in Ancient Israel and the Levant," in *Reflections on the Silence of God: A Discussion with Marjo Korpel and Johannes de Moor* (Leiden: Brill, 2013), 29–31.
12. Korpel and de Moor, *The Silent God*, 67. Marcel Sarot, "Deafening Silence? On Hearing God in the Midst of Suffering," in *Reflections on the Silence of God: A Discussion with Marjo Korpel and Johannes de Moor*, ed. Bob Becking (Leiden: Brill, 2013), 144–149, makes the case that the story of Cain and Abel (Gen 4:1–16) should be added to the texts that explore the silence of God—in this case "regarding" one sacrifice over another.
13. See also Numbers 7:89 for the "voice of God" emanating from the "mercy seat."
14. The word *hārēš* in the *qal* form means "non-hearing" but in the *hiphil* form means "do not be silent." See Sonja Noll, *The Semantics of Silence in Biblical Hebrew* (London: Brill, 2020), 395–396.

15. Sarot, "Deafening Silence," 144. Tony W. Cartledge, *1 & 2 Samuel* (Macon, GA: Smyth & Helwys, 2001), 63.

16. See Hermann Spieckermann, "Schweigen und Beten: Von stillem Lobgesang und zerbrechender Rede im Psalter," in *Das Manna fällt auch heute noch: Beiträge zur Geschichte und Theologie des Alten Testaments: Festschrift für Erich Zenger*, eds. Frank-Lothar Hossfeld and Ludgar Schwienhorst-Schönberger (Freiburg: Herder, 2004), 568–584, for categories of silence in the Psalms.

17. Korpel and de Moor, *The Silent God*, 59. Ellen van Wolde, "A Network of Conventional and Deliberate Metaphors in Psalm 22," *JSOT* 44, no. 4 (2019): 646, makes the case that Psalm 22 can be categorized as both an individual and a collective lament containing both a plea and a reassurance.

18. Compare similar language in Psalm 83:2 and see Noll, *Semantics of Silence*, 54.

19. Frank-Lothar Hossfeld and Erich Zenger, *A Commentary on Psalms 51–100* (Minneapolis: Fortress, 2005), 341.

20. See Lee, *Lyrics of Lament*, 93, for an analysis of the lament form in Psalm 13.

21. Catherine Petrany, "Words Fail Me: Silence, Wisdom, and Liturgy in Psalm 73," *Journal of Theological Interpretation* 13, no. 1 (2019): 115–121, points to the degree of suffering as the basis for human silence rather than addressing the deity.

22. Susanne Gillmayr-Bucher, "Wenn die Dischter verstummen: Das Schweigen in den Psalmen," *Theologie und Glaube* 93 (2003), 317.

23. Robert L. Scott, "Dialectical Tensions of Speaking and Silence," *Quarterly Journal of Speech* 79, no. 1 (1993): 13–15, notes that silence interacts with speech and that each is vital to the other.

24. Baruch A. Levine, "Silence, Sound, and the Phenomenology of Mourning in Biblical Israel," *JANES* 22 (1993): 95–96, sees these expressions of emotion as more typical of mourning practices and silence as a symptom of depression or shock.

25. See Psalm 139:8 and the discussion in Paolo Torresan, "Silence in the Bible," *JBQ* 31, no. 3 (2003): 159.

26. Jürgen Ebach, "Silence in the Bible: A Short Introduction and Seven Miniatures," *Concilium* 5 (2015): 105. See Genesis 50:10 for a similar seven-day ritual.

27. Daniel I. Block, *The Book of Ezekiel, Chapters 1–24* (Grand Rapids, MI: Eerdmans, 1997), 137–141.

28. See John Kessler, *Between Hearing and Silence*, 88.

29. Gillmayr-Bucher, "Wenn die Dischter verstummen," 324–330, points to the silence after death in Psalms 30:9 and 88:11–13, which questions the ability of the dust/the dead to praise God.

30. Victor H. Matthews, *More Than Meets the Ear: Discovering the Hidden Contexts of Old Testament Conversations* (Grand Rapids, MI: Eerdmans, 2008), 67–70.

31. Alan Lenzi, "Invoking the God: Interpreting Invocations in Mesopotamian Prayers and Biblical Laments of the Individual," *JBL* 129, no. 2 (2010), 309, n. 14.

32. Thus, the petitioner is characterized as a "worm" encircled by bulls and dogs while all strength to protect oneself is poured out like water (Ps 22:6–18).

33. Van Wolde, "Metaphors in Psalm 22," 650.

34. Several of the psalms contain overt accusations of God's silence during a crisis. Psalms 22, 44, 74, and 88 all issue an accusation of God's apparent desertion. See Joshua C. Waltman, "Psalms of Lament and God's Silence: Features of Petition Not Yet Answered," *EvQ* 89, no. 3 (2018): 210.

35. Francis I. Andersen and David Noel Freedman, *Amos* (New York: Doubleday, 1989), 823–824, concludes that the "famine" refers to the lack of obedience to the Decalogue and the covenant. It also has a dual meaning indicating both disobedience and divine silence in response.

36. Compare Ezekiel 12:2 and Jeremiah 5:21 for the definition of a rebellious house who "have eyes to see but do not see, who have ears to hear but do not hear."

37. Beau Harris and Carleen Mandolfo, "The Silent God in Lamentations," *Int* 67, no. 2 (2013): 141–143, categorizes YHWH's silence in Lamentations 3 into several categories that include a "respectful silence" in the face of trauma and a "pedagogic silence" that allows for self-reflection to bring about an understanding of why YHWH's punishment was necessary.

38. Brevard S. Childs, *Isaiah* (Louisville, KY: Westminster/John Knox, 2001), 466–467. Paul D. Hanson, *Isaiah 40–66* (Louisville, KY: Westminster/John Knox, 1995), points to the failure of the cult of the restored temple in Jerusalem who have chosen to worship "not Creator but creature."

39. Harris and Mandolfo, "The Silent God," 137. See Kessler, *Between Hearing and Silence*, 107–130, for a fuller examination of the theological implications of God's silence that provides a guide for the role that silence plays in these petitionary passages.

40. Carroll Stuhlmueller, "The Deaf and Silent God of Mysticism and Liturgy," *BTB* 12, no. 3 (1982): 87–88. See the "covering of the lips by seers; for there is no answer from God" (Mic 3:6–7), and the concerns raised about God's silence in Psalm 22:2; 28:1; 29:12 and Habakkuk 1:13.

41. Michael H. Floyd, "Prophetic Complaints about the Fulfillment of Oracles in Habakkuk 1:2–17 and Jeremiah 15:10–18," *JBL* 110, no. 3 (1991): 397–418.

42. The lament form has a long history. The laments over the destruction of Ur date to the period of 2028–2003 BCE and contain the same sense of despair, loss, and dislocation, as well as a cry that their suffering is "enough" to bear. See Matthews and Benjamin, *OTP-5*, 295–302.

43. Compare a similar complaint in Jeremiah 15:10–11.

44. Michael B. Dick, "The Neo-Assyrian Royal Lion Hunt and Yahweh's Answer to Job," *JBL* 125, no. 2 (2006): 263–264, compares this complaint to Neo-Assyrian texts and art.

45. See the discussion of a similar turn to self-reflection in Psalm 73:16 in Petrany, "Words Fail Me," 113–127.

46. Cheryl Glenn, *Unspoken: A Rhetoric Silence* (Carbondale, IL: Southern Illinois University Press, 2004), 9, points out that silence "depends on a power differential" determining who can speak and when.

47. J. Richard Middleton, *Abraham's Silence: The Binding of Isaac, the Suffering of Job, and How to Talk Back to God* (Grand Rapids, MI: Baker Academic, 2021), 76–78, explores the appropriate way to engage in "God-fearing" speech.

48. See Christo Lambaard, "Testing Tales: Genesis 22 and Daniel 3 and 6," in *Prayers and the Construction of Israelite Identity*, eds. Susanne Gillmayr-Bucher and Maria Häusl (Atlanta: SBL, 2019), 114–115.

49. Korpel and de Moor, *The Silent God*, 55.

50. Joel S. Burnett, *Where is God? Divine Absence in the Hebrew Bible* (Minneapolis: Fortress, 2010), 178.

51. Burnett, "Divine Silence or Divine Absence?" 29.

52. Amy Cottrill, *Language, Power, and Identity in the Lament Psalms of the Individual* (London: Continuum, 2008), 1–5. See also Simon P. Stocks, " 'Like the snail that dissolves': Construction of Identity of Psalmist and Enemy in the Lament Psalms of the Individual," *JSOT* 46, no. 1 (20212): 133–143.

53. Israel Knohl, "Between Voice and Silence: The Relationship between Prayer and Temple Cult," *JBL* 115, no. 1 (1996): 27.

54. Adele Berlin, "Hannah and Her Prayers," *Scriptura* 87 (2004): 230–231, contends that the petitioner should not reveal the substance of their petition prior to it being granted. If it is not granted, that would diminish the god's reputation, and if it is granted then the power of the deity would be a reason for celebration. That comes clear in Hannah's second prayer in which she speaks her thanksgiving aloud (1 Sam 2:1–10).

55. Angela K. Harkins, "The Pro-Social Role of Grief in Ezra's Penitential Prayer," *BibInt* 24, no. 4–5 (2016): 466–491.

56. Stephanie Rembold, "Hannah in Stages and Places: An Exploration of Narrative Space in 1 Samuel 1," *OTE* 35, no. 1 (2022): 74–75.

57. Diarmaid MacCulloch, *Silence: A Christian History* (New York: Viking, 2013), 21, suggests that Hannah's silent prayer, while controversial in its original setting, is the justification of the practice in later Judaism and Christianity. Thus, the admonition in Matt 6:6–7 to pray in your closet may be an extension of this principle, but it also serves as the contrast to those whose prayers and worship practices are ineffectual—see Amos 4:4–5.

58. Pieter W. van der Horst, "Silent Prayer in Antiquity," *Numen* 41, no. 1 (1992): 1–2, notes that within Greek and Latin sources before the Christian era, prayers were spoken out loud based on an anthropomorphic belief that the deity had ears and therefore a silent prayer would remain unheard. He also suggests (pp. 13–14), citing Pseudo-Philo, that the reason for Hannah's silent prayer is to prevent her co-wife from hearing her words and taunting her.

59. Hannes Bezzel, "Hannah's Prayer(s) in 1 Samuel 1–2 and in Pseudo-Philo's Liber *antiquitatum biblicarum*," in *Prayers and the Construction of Israelite Identity*, eds. Susanne Gillmayr-Bucher and Maria Häusl (Atlanta: SBL, 2019), 150.

60. For Berlin, "Hannah and Her Prayers," 230, Eli's misunderstanding makes perfect sense because ancient prayer was not supposed to be silent.

61. Justin Jackson, "The Bows of the Mighty are Broken: The 'Fall' of the Proud and the Exaltation of the Humble in 1 Samuel," *Themelios* 46, no. 2 (2021): 291–293, sees the reversal of authoritative stance between Hannah and Eli as the opening example of a pattern in 1 Samuel.

62. Rembold, "Hannah in Stages and Places," 77. See Serge Frolov, *The Turn of the Cycle: 1 Samuel 1–9 in Synchronic and Diachronic Perspectives* (Berlin: Walter de Gruyter, 2004), 88–89, for the suggestion that Eli's

quick blessing may be an attempt to send her on her way and to cover his embarrassment.

63. J. Gerald Janzen, "Prayer and/as Self-Address: The Case of Hannah," in *A God So Near: Essays on Old Testament Theology in Honor of Patrick D. Miller*, eds. Brent A. Strawn and Nancy R. Bowen (Winona Lake, IN: Eisenbrauns, 2003), 113.

64. See also Psalm 62:1, 5 and Psalm 37:7.

65. Note that this does not negate the necessity for repentance to receive YHWH's forgiveness (Ps 32:3). Noll, *Semantics of Silence*, 24, suggests that the penitent in this psalm is not keeping complete silence but is groaning without making a confession of sin.

66. Scott C. Jones, "Psalm 37 and the Devotionalization of Instruction in the Postexilic Period," in *Prayers and the Construction of Israelite Identity*, eds. Susanne Gillmayr-Bucher and Maria Häusl (Atlanta: SBL, 2019), 167–187.

67. Kessler, *Between Hearing and Silence*, 75.

68. Noll, *Semantics of Silence*, 128. Norris J. Chumley, *Be Still and Know: God's Presence in Silence* (Minneapolis: Fortress Press, 2014), 1, refers to this practice with the Greek word *hesychia* as a method of controlling the body and focusing the mind through quietude and prayer.

69. C. J. Labuschagne, "The Metaphor of the So-Called 'Weaned Child' in Psalm cxxxi," *VT* 57, no. 1 (2007): 117–118, makes a good case for translating here a "breast-fed suckling, quieted and satisfied" rather than a "weaned child."

70. Kessler, *Between Hearing and Silence*, 75–76.

71. Andre D. Neher, "Speech and Silence in Prophecy," *Dor le Dor* 6, no. 2 (1977–78): 64, sees the lack of response by YHWH to Saul's query as a divine "evasion" that also is an answer.

72. See Rhiannon Graybill, "Hear and Give Ear!: The Soundscape of Jeremiah," *JSOT* 40, no. 4 (2016): 486, on the dread caused by God's silence.

73. See Victor A. Hurowitz, "True Light on the Urim and Thummim," *JQR* 88, no. 3–4 (1998): 263–268, for a review of Cornelis van Dam, *The Urim and Thummim: A Means of Revelation in Ancient Israel* (Winona Lake, IN: Eisenbrauns, 1997), and his refutation of van Dam's thesis that they were a single object that worked through the person of the High Priest and communicated by emitting a light pulse.

74. Cornelis Houtman, "The Urim and Thummim: A New Suggestion," *VT* 40, no. 2 (1990): 231, interprets the requirement that the High

Priest must bear the Urim and Thummim "upon his heart" (Exod 28:29) as evidence for an emanation from them, causing the priest to speak the divine response.

75. Burnett, "Divine Silence or Divine Absence?" 32–33.
76. Waltman, "Psalms of Lament," 210.
77. Victor H. Matthews, "Theophanies Cultic and Cosmic: 'Prepare to Meet Thy God!' " in *Israel's Apostasy and Restoration: Essays in Honor of Roland K. Harrison*, ed. Avraham Gileadi (Grand Rapids, MI: Baker, 1988), 307–317.
78. Jack M. Sasson, "Oracle Inquiries in Judges," in *Birkat Shalom: Ancient Near Eastern Literature and Postbiblical Judaism Presented to Shalom M. Paul on the Occasion of His Seventieth Birthday*, ed. Chaim Cohen, et al (Winona Lake, IN: Eisenbrauns, 2008), 165–168.
79. Stephen C. Russell, "Samuel's Theophany and the Politics of Religious Dreams," in *Perchance to Dream: Dream Divination in the Bible and the Ancient Near East*, eds. Esther Hamori and Jonathan Stökl (Atlanta: SBL, 2018), 111–116, details the shared features of dream theophanies in the biblical text and ancient Near Eastern literature.
80. Jesse Rainbow, "Micaiah be Imlah (1 Kings 22) and the Grammar of the Biblical War Oracle," *JBL* 138, no. 3 (2019): 539–541.
81. Victor H. Matthews, *Experiencing Scripture: The Five Senses in Biblical Interpretation* (Minneapolis: Fortress, 2023), 100–101.
82. Joanna Stiebert, "The Body and Voice of God in the Hebrew Bible," *Journal for Religion, Film and Media* 2, no. 1 (2016): 29–30.
83. Moshe Weinfeld, *Deuteronomy 1–11* (New York: Doubleday, 1991), 324, notes that the people are simply placing Moses into the position as go-between. Up to now, they had "managed to hear the voice of YHWH and survived."
84. Korpel and de Moor, *The Silent God*, 35, has compiled 1,882 verbs and nouns that refer to divine speech and just 29 verbs and nouns that refer directly to divine silence.
85. That may be the case when a period passes after Hananiah breaks the yoke off Jeremiah's neck and pronounces an end to Babylonian aggression (Jer 28:10–12). Jeremiah is only reenergized to speak after that pause in communication.
86. Gershon Hepner, "Three's a Crowd in Shunem: Elisha's Misconduct with the Shunammite Reflects a Polemic against Prophetism," *ZAW* 122, no. 3 (2010): 397–399, suggests that Elisha is the one who fathers the woman's child as part of a "tripartite breeding" practice since the husband is unable to father a child.

87. Keeping information "hidden" from a prophet is unusual since it is more common for YHWH to divulge critical data prior to an event. See 1 Samuel 9:15 and 1 Kings 14:5.

88. Yairah Amit, "A Prophet Tested: Elisha, the Great Woman of Shunem, and the Story's Double Message," *BibInt* 11, no. 3–4 (2003): 291–292.

89. That comes clear in the unnecessary use of Gehazi as an intercessor, something that kings are more prone to do rather than deal with supplicants personally. See the discussion in Mark Roncace, "Elisha and the Woman of Shunem: 2 Kings 4.8–37 and 8:1–6 Read in Conjunction," *JSOT* 25, no. 91 (2000): 111–115.

90. Tod Linafelt, "Speech and Silence in the Servant Passages: Towards a Final-Form Reading of the Book of Isaiah," *Koinonia* 5, no. 2 (1993): 180, points to a silent servant in Isaiah 42 because "the nation has yet to assume its role as the one who speaks rightly about YHWH." But that silence is to be broken in Isaiah 42:10 where Israel is to "sing to the Lord a new song, his praise from the end of the earth!" in contrast to the false gods, who are incapable of speech (Isa 41:21–28).

91. Linafelt, "Speech and Silence in the Servant Passages," 176.

92. While not commanding silence, other passages call for a close listening to the speech of YHWH: Isaiah 42:23; 44:1, 46:3, 12; 48:1, 14; 51:1, 4.

93. See Coralie A. Gutridge, "The Sacrifice of Fools and the Wisdom of Silence: Qoheleth, Job and the Presence of God," in *Biblical Hebrews, Biblical texts: Essays in Memory of Michael P. Weitzman*, eds. Ada Rapoport-Albert and Gillian Greenberg (London; New York: Sheffield Academic Press, 2001), 83–99.

94. Compare Miller, "Silence as a Response," 36, who considers that "silence by the deity is uniformly represented as the absence of a response."

95. Korpel and de Moor, *Silent God*, 66, n. 36; and Van Elferen and Raeymaekers, "Silent Dark," 262.

96. See Eric D. Reymond, "The Hebrew Word *damah* and the Root d-m-m ("To be Silent")," *Biblica* 90, no. 3 (2009): 377–378.

97. Samuel E. Balentine, *Job* (Macon, GA: Smyth & Helwys, 2006), 392–394, sees the "whisper" as the total of what humanity can discern of creation and its workings.

98. Glenn, *Unspoken: A Rhetoric of Silence*, 4, describes silence in mathematical terms equating it with zero, which has both an integral and rhetorical function.

99. They also appear elsewhere during the seventh plague in Egypt and are marked by thunder and damaging hail. Significantly, all these

manifestations of natural violence cease when Moses calls on God to end the plague (Exod 9:29–33).

100. See Ebach, "Silence in the Bible," 106–107, for various translations of the Hebrew phrase *Qōl d'mama daqqa*. Gören Eidevall, "Sounds of Silence in Biblical Hebrew: A Lexical Study," *VT* 62, no. 2 (2012): 172, translates *děmāmâ* as "a fine sound of stillness" that comes after the turmoil had ceased. This same word is used in Job 4:16 as a "whisper" or a "silence" prior to a divine voice speaking. Reymond, "The Hebrew Word *damah*," 378–379, makes the case for "how a word or root associated with silence can modify a word associated with sound or speech"— compare with Psalm 32:3.

101. Noll, *The Semantics of Silence*, 197–201. Benjamin, *The Social World of Deuteronomy*, 1, sees the contrast in voice to be reflection of YHWH as a "male warrior who puts the powerful to death" and a "female mourner who laments over those who have been slain.

102. Jack Bilmes, "Constituting Silence: Life in the World of Total Meaning," *Semiotica* 98, no. 1–2 (1994): 73–74, refers to a corresponding 'anti-thing,' as an absence."

103. Scott, "Dialectical Tensions of Speaking and Silence," 11.

104. Michal Ephratt, *Silence as Language: Verbal Silence as a Means of Expression* (Cambridge: Cambridge, 2022), 6, points out that kinetic stillness and acoustic stillness can combine to create absolute silence/stillness.

105. See Sigve Tonstad, "The limits of power: revisiting Elijah and Horeb," SJOT 19, no. 2 (2005): 253–266. Bernard P. Robinson, "Elijah at Horeb, 1 Kings 19:1–18: a Coherent Narrative?" *RB* 98, no. 4 (1991): 520–521, differentiates YHWH's presence from the "still small voice."

106. See Brian Britt, "Prophetic Concealment in a Biblical Type Scene," *CBQ* 64, no. 1 (2002): 37–58.Max Rogland, "Elijah and the 'Voice' at Horeb (1 Kings 19): Narrative Sequence in the Masoretic Text and Josephus," *VT* 62, no. 1 (2012): 92–94, restructures the translation, bringing it closer to the account in Josephus (A.J. 8.13.7 §§349–352) and suggests that the first set of powerful images do not constitute a theophany. Only the silence marks God's presence.

107. The Hebrew phrase is *qol deṁ āma daqqa*.

108. Note that that this same word is translated in Job 4:12–16 as a "whisper" or a moment of "silence" prior to a divine voice speaking. See J. Lust, "A Gentle Breeze or a Roaring Thunderous Sound? Elijah at Horeb: 1 Kings XIX 12," *VT* 25, no. 1 (1975): 110–115.

109. Note Jesus's calming of the storm on the Sea of Galilee, saying only "Peace! Be Still!" and generating awe and the recognition of great

power by the disciples (Mark 4:35–41). On this passage, see Elizabeth Struthers Malbon, "The Jesus of Mark and the Sea of Galilee," *JBL* 103, no. 3 (1984): 365–366.

110. John A. Beck, "Geography as Irony: The Narrative-Geographical Shaping of Elijah's Duel with the Prophets of Baal (1 Kings 18)," *SJOT* 17, no. 2 (2003): 296–298.

111. See Amos 1:2 when YHWH chooses to allow pasture lands to wither and the top of Mt. Carmel to dry up.

112. Nadav Na'aman, "The Contest on Mount Carmel (1 Kings 18:19–40) as a Reflection of a Religious-Cultural Threat," *BZ* 64, no. 1 (2020): 90–92, sees this story as a response to the cultural and political incursion of the Persians during the post-exilic period with an aim to provide a monotheistic message detailing the exclusive power of YHWH and the fallacy of belief in any other god.

113. Neil Glover, "Elijah versus the Narrative of Elijah: The Contest between the Prophet and the Word," *JSOT* 30, no. 4 (2006): 451.

114. Miller, "Silence as a Response," 34, suggests it is also a way to save Elijah the embarrassment of a refusal.

115. Gary Rendsburg, "The Mock of Baal in 1 Kings 18:27," *CBQ* 50, no. 3 (1988): 414–417, using comparable Semitics to suggest that "meditating" should be rendered "urinating/defecating" as the basis of Ba'al's inattention. Such an anthropomorphic aspect reduces Ba'al's divine character.

116. Andrzej Mrozek, "The Motif of the Sleeping Divinity," *CBQ* 80, no. 3 (1999): 418, points to the Mesopotamian epic of Atrahasis in which the god Enki is asleep and must be awoken to deal with a rebellion by the other gods.

117. Bernard F. Batto, "When God Sleeps," *Bible Review* 3, no. 4 (1987): 19–21, points to Isaiah 51:9–11 and the cry of the exilic community for YHWH to "Awake!" as evidence that YHWH is giving no thought to them and his arch enemy, Rahab, is being given an opening to challenge him.

118. Batto, "When God Sleeps," 22.

119. What Miller, "Silence as a Response," 37, refers to as a "zero sign."

120. Hossfeld and Zenger, *Psalms 51–100*, 325.

121. Scott, "Dialectical Tensions of Speaking and Silence," 12–13, points to three forms of silence as part of the communication process: (1) attentive silence, (2) terminal silence, and (3) silences that punctuate.

BIBLIOGRAPHY

Acheson, Kris. "Silence as Gesture: Rethinking the Nature of Communicative Silence." *Communication Theory* 18, no. 4 (2008): 535–555.

Achino-Loeb, Maria-Luisa. "Introduction." In *Silence: The Currency of Power*, edited by Maria-Luisa Achino-Loeb, 1–19. New York: Berghahn Books, 2006.

Adamo, David. "The Unheard Voices in the Hebrew Bible: The Nameless and Silent Wife of Jeroboam (1 Kgs 14:1–18)." *OTE* 33, no. 3 (2020): 393–407.

Alexander, T. Desmond. "Lot's Hospitality: A Clue to His Righteousness." *JBL* 104, no. 2 (1985): 289–291.

Alter, Robert. *The Art of Biblical Narrative*. New York: Basic Books, 1981.

Amit, Yairah. "A Prophet Tested: Elisha, the Great Woman of Shunem, and the Story's Double Message." *BibInt* 11, no. 3–4 (2003): 279–294.

Amzallag, Nissim and Shamir Yona. "The Kenite Origin of the Sotah Prescription (Numbers 5.11–31)." *JSOT* 41, no. 4 (2017): 383–412.

Andersen, Francis I. and David Noel Freedman. *Amos*. New York: Doubleday, 1989.

Auld, A. Graeme. *I & II Samuel: A Commentary*. Louisville, KY: Westminster/ John Knox, 2011.

Bailey, Randall C. *David in Love and War: The Pursuit of Power in 2 Samuel 10–12*. Sheffield, England: JSOT Press, 1990.

Balentine, Samuel E. *Job*. Macon, GA: Smyth & Helwys, 2006.

Bannester, E. Michael. "Sociodynamics: An Integrative Theorem of Power, Authority, Interfluence and Love." *American Sociological Review* 34, no. 3 (1969): 374–393.

Bar-Efrat, Shimon. *Narrative Art in the Bible*. Sheffield, England: Almond Press, 1989.

Batto, Bernard F. "When God Sleeps." *Bible Review* 3, no. 4 (1987): 16–23.

Bauer, Uwe F. W. "Judges 19 as an Anti-Spy Story in the Context of an Anti-Conquest Story: The Creative Usage of Literary Genres." *JSOT* 88 (2000): 37–47.

Beach, Bradley and Matthew T. Powell, eds. *Interpreting Abraham: Journeys to Moriah* Minneapolis: Fortress, 2014.

Beck, John A. "Geography as Irony: The Narrative-Geographical Shaping of Elijah's Duel with The Prophets of Baal (1 Kings 18)." *SJOT* 17, no. 2 (2003): 291–302.

Bednarowski, K. Paul. "Surprise and Suspense in Aeschylus' *Agamemnon*." *American Journal of Philology* 136, no. 2 (2015): 179–205.

Beeman, William O. "Silence in Music." In *Silence: The Currency of Power*, edited by Maria-Luisa Achino-Loeb, 23–34. New York: Berghahn Books, 2006.

Bembry, Jason. "The Levite's Concubine (Judg 19:2) and the Tradition of Sexual Slander in the Hebrew Bible: How the Nature of Her Departure Illustrates a Tradition's Tendency." *VT* 68, no. 4 (2018): 519–539.

Ben Zvi, Ehud. "Who Wrote the Speech of Rabshakeh and When?" *JBL* 109, no. 1 (1990): 79–92.

Benjamin, Don C. *The Social World of Deuteronomy: A New Feminist Commentary*. Cambridge: James Clarke & Co., 2017.

———. *The Old Testament Story, an Introduction*. Minneapolis: Fortress, 2004.

Berlin, Adele. "Hannah and Her Prayers." *Scriptura* 87 (2004): 227–232.

Bezzel, Hannes. "Hannah's Prayer(s) in 1 Samuel 1–2 and in Pseudo-Philo's *Liber antiquitatum Biblicarum*." In *Prayers and the Construction of Israelite Identity*, edited by Susanne Gillmayr-Bucher and Maria Häusl, 147–164. Atlanta: SBL, 2019.

Bilmes, Jack. "Constituting Silence: Life in the World of Total Meaning." *Semiotica* 98, no. 1–2 (1994): 73–87.

Blenkinsopp, Joseph. *Isaiah 40–55*. New York: Doubleday, 2002.

Block, Daniel I. *The Book of Ezekiel, Chapters 1–24*. Grand Rapids, MI: Eerdmans, 1997.

Boase, Elizabeth and Sarah Agnew. " 'Whispered in the Sound of Silence': Traumatizing the Book of Jonah." *The Bible & Critical Theory* 12, no. 1 (2016): 4–22.

Bodner, Keith. *Jeroboam's Royal Drama*. Oxford: Oxford, 2012.

Boehm, Omri. *The Binding of Isaac: A Religious Model of Disobedience*. New York: T&T Clark, 2007.

———. "Child Sacrifice, Ethical Responsibility and the Existence of the People of Israel." *VT* 54, no. 2 (2004): 145–156.

Booth, Wayne C. *The Knowing Most Worth Doing*. Charlottesville, VA: University of Virginia Press, 2010.

———. *The Essential Wayne Booth*, edited by Walter Jost. Chicago: University of Chicago Press, 2006).

———. "Where is the Authorial Audience in Biblical Narrative—and in Other 'Authoritative' Texts?" *Narrative* 4, no. 3 (1996): 235–253.

———. *The Rhetoric of Fiction*, 2nd ed. Chicago: Chicago, 1983.

Bosworth, David A. "Daughter Zion and Weeping in Lamentations 1–2." *JSOT* 38, no. 2 (2013): 217–237.

Bovati, Pietro. *Re-Establishing Justice: Legal Terms, Concepts and Procedures in the Hebrew Bible*. Sheffield, England: JSOT Press, 1994.

Branch, Robin G. *Jeroboam's Wife: The Enduring Contributions of the Old Testament's Least-Known Women*. Peabody, MA: Hendrickson, 2009.

———. "The Wife of Jeroboam, 1 Kings 14:1–18: The Incredible, Riveting, History-Changing Significance of an Unnamed, Overlooked, Ignored, Obscure, Obedient Woman." *OTE* 17, no. 2 (2004): 157–167.

Brenner, Athalya. "Introduction." In *A Feminist Companion to Judges*, edited by Athalya Brenner, 9–22. Sheffield, England: JSOT Press, 1993.

———. "Rizpah [Re]membered: 2 Samuel 1–14 and Beyond." In *Performing Memory in Biblical Narrative and Beyond*, edited by Athalya Brenner and Frank H. Polak, 207–227. Sheffield, England: Sheffield Phoenix Press, 2009.

Brett, Mark G. "Abraham's 'Heretical' Imperative: A Response to Jacques Derrida." In *The Meanings We Choose: Hermeneutical Ethics, Indeterminacy and the Conflict of Interpretations*, edited by Charles H. Cosgrove, 166–178. London: T & T Clark, 2004.

———. *Genesis: Procreation and the Politics of Identity*. London: Routledge, 2000.

Brettler, Marc Z. "(Divine) Silence is Golden: A New Reading of the Prologue of Job." In *Interested Readers: Essays on the Hebrew Bible in Honor of David J. A. Clines*, edited by James K. Aitken, Jeremy M.S. Clines, and Christi M. Maier, 19–26. Atlanta: SBL, 2013.

Britt, Brian. "Male Jealousy and the Suspected *Sotah*: Toward a Counter-Reading of Numbers 5:11–31." *The Bible & Critical Theory* 3, no. 1 (2007): 1–19.

———. "Death, social conflict, and the barley harvest in the Hebrew Bible." *JHS* 5 (2004–2005): http://www.purl.org/jhs.

———. "Prophetic Concealment in a Biblical Type Scene." *CBQ* 64, no. 1 (2002): 37–58.

Brummett, Barry. "Towards a Theory of Silence as a Political Strategy." *The Quarterly Journal of Speech* 66, no. 3 (1980): 289–303.

Burnett, Joel S. "Divine Silence or Divine Absence? Converging Metaphors in Family Religion in Ancient Israel and the Levant." In *Reflections on the Silence of God: A Discussion with Marjo Korpel and Johannes de Moor*, edited by Bob Becking, 29–70. Leiden: Brill, 2013.

———. *Where is God? Divine Absence in the Hebrew Bible*. Minneapolis: Fortress, 2010.

Carden, Michael. "Genesis/*Bereshit*." In *The Queer Bible Commentary*, edited by Deryn Guest, et al, 21–60. London: SCM Press, 2006.

Carroll, Robert P. *Jeremiah*. Philadelphia: Westminster, 1986.

Cartledge, Tony W. *1 & 2 Samuel*. Macon, GA: Smyth & Helwys, 2001.

Carvalho (Patton), Corrine L. "From Heroic Individual to Nameless Victim: Women in the Social World of the Judges." In *Biblical and Humane: A Festschrift for John F. Priest*, edited by Linda Elder, David L. Barr, and Elizbeth Struthers, 33–46. Atlanta: Scholars Press, 1996.

Case, Megan L. "Michal the Giver and Michal the Taker: The Systematic Misogyny of the Davidic Court." *BibInt* 31, no. 1 (2023): 25–43.

Chavel, Simeon. "Compositry and Creativity in 2 Samuel 21:1–14." *JBL* 122, no. 1 (2003): 23–52.

Childs, Brevard S. *Isaiah*. Louisville, KY: Westminster/John Knox, 2001.

Chumley, Norris J. *Be Still and Know: God's Presence in Silence*. Minneapolis: Fortress Press, 2014.

Cifers, Carrie. "She Decides: Reading Genesis 34 in Conversation with Narrative Ethics." *Int* 77, no. 1 (2023): 52–60.

Clair, Robin P. *Organizing Silence*. Albany, NY: State University of New York Press, 1998.

Clines, David J.A. "David the Man: The Construction of Masculinity in the Hebrew Bible." In *Interested Parties: The Ideology of Writers and Readers of the Hebrew Bible*, edited by David J. A. Clines, 212–241. JSOTSup, 205; Gender, Culture, Theory 1; Sheffield, England: Sheffield Academic, 1995.

Cloud, Dana L. "The Null Persona: Race and the Rhetoric of Silence in the Uprising of '34." *Rhetoric & Public Affairs* 2, no. 2 (1999): 177–209.

Coats, George W. "Lot: A Foil in the Abraham Saga." In *Understanding the Word: Essays in Honor of Bernhard W. Anderson*, edited by James T. Butler, et al., 113–132. JSOTSup 37; Sheffield, England: JSOT Press, 1985.

Cobb, Kirsi. "Did Lot Get His Just Desserts? Trauma, Revenge, and Re-enactment in Genesis 19.30–38." *JSOT* 47, no. 2 (2022): 189–205.

———. "'Look at What They've Turned Us Into': Reading the Story of Lot's Daughters with Trauma Theory and *The Handmaid's Tale*." *Open Theology* 7 (2021): 208–223.

Cohn, Robert L. "Literary Technique in the Jeroboam Narrative." *ZAW* 97, no. 1 (1985): 23–35.

Coogan, Michael D. and Mark S. Smith. *Stories from Ancient Canaan*, 2nd ed. Louisville, KY: Westminster/John Knox, 2012.

Cook, Stephen L. "The Speechless Suppression of Grief in Ezekiel 24:15–27: The Death of Ezekiel's Wife and the Prophet's Abnormal Response." In *Thus Says the Lord: Essays on the Former and Latter Prophets in Honor of Robert R. Wilson*, edited by John J. Ahn and Stephen L. Cook, 222–233. New York: T & T Clark, 2009.

Cottrill, Amy. *Language, Power, and Identity in the Lament Psalms of the Individual*. London: Continuum, 2008.

Craig, Kenneth M. "Rhetorical Aspects of Questions Answered with Silence in 1 Samuel 12:37 and 28:6." *CBQ* 56, no. 2 (1994): 221–239.

Crotty, Robert. "The Literary Structure of the Binding of Isaac in Genesis 22." *ABR* 53 (2005): 31–41.

Cryer, Frederick H. "David's Rise to Power and the Death of Abner: An Analysis of 1 Samuel XXVI 14–16 and Its Redaction-Critical Implications." *VT* 35, no. 4 (1985): 385–394.

Dambska, Izydora. "Silence as an Expression and as a Value." In *Knowledge, Language and Silence: Selected Papers*, edited by Anna Brozek and Jacek Jadacki, 311–318. Leiden: Brill, 2016.

Das, Dee. "Silence in Literary Fiction." (2022): https://bookriot.com/silence-in-literary-fiction/.

Dauenhauer, Bernard P. *Silence: The Phenomenon and Its Ontological Significance*. Bloomington, IN: Indiana University Press, 1980.

Day, Linda. "Rhetoric and Domestic Violence in Ezekiel 16." *BibInt* 8, no. 3 (2000): 205–230.

Deken, Alice. "Does Prophecy Cause History? Jeremiah 36: A Scroll Ablaze." *OTE* 30, no. 3 (2017): 630–652.

Derrida, Jacques. *A Taste for the Secret*. Cambridge: Polity Press, 2001.

Dick, Michael S. "The Neo-Assyrian Royal Lion Hunt and Yahweh's Answer to Job." *JBL* 125, no. 2 (2006): 243–270.

Dinkler, Michael B. *Silent Statements: Narrative Representations of Speech and Silence in the Gospel of Luke*. Doctoral Dissertation; Cambridge: Harvard Divinity School, 2012.

Dobbs-Allsopp, F. W. "R(az/ais)ing Zion in Lamentations 2." In *David and Zion: Biblical Studies in Honor of J. J. M. Roberts*, edited by Bernard Batto and Kathryn L. Roberts, 21–68. Winona Lake, IN: Eisenbrauns, 2004.

Dozeman, Thomas B. "The Wilderness and Salvation History in the Hagar Story." *JBL* 117, no. 1 (1998): 23–43.

Dragojlovic, Ana and Annemarie Samuels. "Tracing Silences: Toward and Anthropology of the Unspoken and Unspeakable." *History & Anthropology* 32, no. 4 (2021): 417–425.

Dutcher-Walls, Patricia. *Narrative Art, Political Rhetoric: The Case of Athaliah and Joash.* Sheffield, England: Sheffield Academic Press, 1996.

Ebach, Jurgen. "Silence in the Bible: A Short Introduction and Seven Miniatures." *Concilium* 5 (2015): 104–113.

Ebert, Teresa. *Ludic Feminism and After: Postmodernism, Desire, and Labor in Late Capitalism.* Ann Arbor, MI: University of Michigan Press, 1996.

Eichler, Raanan. "A Sin is Borne: Clearing up the Law of Women's Vows (Numbers 30)." *VT* 71, no. 3 (2021): 317–328.

Eidevall, Gören. "Sounds of Silence in Biblical Hebrew: A Lexical Study." *VT* 62, no. 2 (2012): 159–174.

———. "Horeb Revisited: Reflections on the Theophany in 1 Kings 19." In *Enigmas and Images: Studies in Honor of Tryggve N. D. Mettinger*, edited by Gören Eidevall and Blaženka Scheuer, 92–111. Winona Lake: Eisenbrauns, 2011.

Eischelbach, Michael A. *Has Joab Foiled David? A Literary Study of the Importance of Joab's Character in Relation to David.* New York: Peter Lang, 2005.

Enninger, Werner. "Focus on Silence Across Cultures." *Intercultural Communication Studies* 1, no. 1 (1991): 1–37.

Ephratt, Michal. *Silence as Language: Verbal Silence as a Means of Expression.* Cambridge: Cambridge University Press, 2022.

———. "The Functions of Silence." *Journal of Pragmatics* 40 (2008): 1909–1938.

Exum, J. Cheryl. *Fragmented Women: Feminist (Sub)versions of Biblical Narratives.* Valley Forge, PA: Trinity Press International, 1993.

Firth, David G. "David and Uriah (With an Occasional Appearance by Uriah's Wife): Reading and Re-Reading 2 Samuel 11." *OTE* 21, no. 2 (2008): 310–328.

Fleishman, Joseph. "Legal Innovation in Deuteronomy XXI 18–20." *VT* 53, no. 3 (2003): 311–327.

Floyd, Michael H. "Prophetic Complaints about the Fulfillment of Oracles in Habakkuk 1:2–17 and Jeremiah 15:10–18." *JBL* 110, no. 3 (1991): 397–418.

Foreman, Benjamin. "Strike the Tongue: Silencing the Prophet in Jeremiah 18:18b." *VT* 59, no. 4 (2009): 653–657.

Foster, Stuart J. " 'Hey, you! Job! Listen up.' Elihu's Use of Job's Name and Its Implications for Translation." *OTE* 29, no. 3 (2016): 455–468.

Frechette, Christopher G. *Mesopotamian Ritual-prayers of "Hand-lifting" (Akkadian šuillas): An Investigation of Function in Light of the Idiomatic Meaning of the Rubric.* Münster, Germany: Ugarit-Verlag, 2012.

Freeden, Michael. "Silence in Political Theory: A Conceptual Predicament," *Journal of Political Ideologies* 20, no. 1 (2015): 1–9.

Friebel, Kelvin G. *Jeremiah's and Ezekiel's Sign-Acts: Rhetorical Nonverbal Communication.* JSOT Sup. 283; Sheffield, England: Sheffield University Press, 1999.

Frolov, Serge. *The Turn of the Cycle: 1 Samuel 1—9 in Synchronic and Diachronic Perspectives.* Berlin: Walter de Gruyter, 2004.

Frolov, Serge, and Vladimir Orel. "Rizpah on the Rock: Notes on 2 Sam. 21:1–14." *Bibbia e Oriente* 37, no. 3 (1995): 145–154.

Frymer-Kensky, Tikva. "The Strange Case of the Suspected Sotah (Numbers V 11–31)." *VT* 34, no. 1 (1984): 11–26.

Fuchs, Esther. "The Literary Characterization of Mothers and the Sexual Politics in the Hebrew Bible." In *Women in the Hebrew Bible: A Reader,* edited by Alice Bach, 117–136. New York: Routledge, 1999.

Geobey, Ronald A. "The Jeroboam Story in the (Re)Formulation of Israelite Identity: Evaluating the Literary-Ideological Purposes of 1 Kings 11–14," *JHS* 16, no. 2 (2016): https://jhsonline.org/index.php/jhs/.

Gerstenberger, Erhard S. *Leviticus.* Louisville: Westminster/John Knox, 1996.

Geyer, John B. *Mythology and Lament: Studies in the Oracles About the Nations.* Burlington, VT: Ashgate Publishing, 20004.

Gillmayr-Bucher, Susanne. "Wenn die Dischter verstummen: Das Schweigen in den Psalmen." *Theologie und Glaube* 93 (2003): 316–332.

Glanville, Mark. "The *Gĕr* (Stranger) in Deuteronomy: Family for the Displace." *JBL* 137, no. 3 (2018): 599–623.

Glenn, Cheryl. *Unspoken: A Rhetoric of Silence.* Carbondale, IL: Southern Illinois University Press, 2004.

Glover, Neil. "Elijah versus the Narrative of Elijah: The Contest between the Prophet and the Word." *JSOT* 30, no. 4 (2006): 449–462.

Goldingay, John. "What Happens to Ms Babylon in Isaiah 47, Why, and Who Says So." *TynBul* 47, no. 2 (1996): 215–243.

Goldzwig, Stephen R. "Demagoguery, Democratic Dissent, and 'Re-Visioning' Democracy." *Rhetoric & Public Affairs* 9, no. 3 (2006): 471–478.

Gravett, Emily O. "The Risk of Retelling: Gomer-bat-Diblaim, Biblical Retrieval, and the Male Gaze in the Prophet's Wife." *BibInt* 27, no. 3 (2019): 436–461.

Graybill, Rhiannon. "Hear and Give Ear! The Soundscape of Jeremiah." *JSOT* 40, no. 4 (2016): 467–490.

Grossman, Jonathan. " 'Associative Meanings' in the Character Evaluation of Lot's Daughters." *CBQ* 76, no. 1 (2104): 40–57.

Gutridge, Coralie A. "The Sacrifice of Fools and the Wisdom of Silence: Qoheleth, Job and the Presence of God." In *Biblical Hebrews, Biblical Texts: Essays in Memory of Michael P. Weitzman*, edited by Ada Rapoport-Albert and Gillian Greenberg, 83–99. London; New York: Sheffield Academic Press, 2001.

Haigh, Rebekah. "Silencing the Land: Joshua as a Military Ritualist." *BibInt* 31, no. 2 (2023): 158–178.

Halpern, Baruch. *David's Secret Demons: Messiah, Murderer, Traitor, King*. Grand Rapids, MI: Eerdmans, 2001.

Hamley, Isabelle. " 'Dis(re)membered and Unaccounted For': פילגש in the Hebrew Bible." *JSOT* 42, no. 4 (2018): 415–434.

Hanson, Paul D. *Isaiah 40–66*. Louisville, KY: Westminster/John Knox, 1995.

Harding, James E. "Homophobia and Masculine Domination in Judges 19—21." *The Bible and Critical Theory* 12, no. 2 (2016): 41–74.

Harkins, Angela K. "The Pro-Social Role of Grief in Ezra's Penitential Prayer." *BibInt* 24, no. 4–5 (2016): 466–491.

Harris, Beau and Carleen Mandolfo. "The Silent God in Lamentations." *Int* 67, no. 2 (2013): 133–143.

Hartley, John E. *Leviticus*. Dallas, TX: Word Books, 1992.

Häusl, Maria. "Women at the King's Court: Their Political, Economic, and Religious Significance in the Accounts of the Former Prophets." In *Prophecy and Gender in the Hebrew Bible*, edited by Juliana Claassens, 229–252. Atlanta: SBL, 2021.

Hawk, L. Daniel. *Joshua*. Collegeville, MN: Liturgical Press, 2000.

Heard, R. Chistopher. *Dynamics of Diselection: Ambiguity in Genesis 12–36 and Ethnic Boundaries in Post-Exilic Judah*. Semeia 39; Atlanta: SBL, 2001.

Hendel, Ronald S., Chana Kronfeld, and Ilana Pardes. "Gender and Sexuality." In *Reading Genesis: Ten Methods*, edited by Ron Hendel, 71–91. Cambridge: Cambridge University Press, 2010.

Hens-Piazza, Gina. *1–2 Kings*. Nashville: Abingdon, 2006.

Hepner, Gershon. "Three's a Crowd in Shunem: Elisha's Misconduct with the Shunammite Reflects a Polemic against Prophetism." *ZAW* 122, no. 3 (2010): 387–400.

Heth, Raleigh C. "Isaac and Iphigenia: Portrayals of Child Sacrifice in Israelite and Greek Literature." *Biblica* 104, no. 2 (2021): 481–502.

Hibbard, J. Todd. "True and False Prophecy: Jeremiah's Revision of Deuteronomy." *JSOT* 35, no. 3 (2011): 339–358.

Higgins, Ryan S. "He Would not Hear Her Voice: From Skilled Speech to Silence in 2 Samuel 13:1–22." *Journal of Feminist Studies in Religion* 36, no. 2 (2020): 25–42.

Hildebrandt, Samuel. "When Words Become Too Violent: Silence as a Form of Nonviolent Resistance in the Book of Jeremiah." *BibInt* 29, no. 2 (2021): 187–205.

Holder, John. "The Presuppositions, Accusations, and Threats of 1 Kings 14:1–18." *JBL* 107, no. 1 (1988): 27–38.

Holladay, William A. *Jeremiah 2*. Minneapolis: Fortress, 1989.

Holt, Else K. "Word of Jeremiah—Word of God: Structures of Authority in the Book of Jeremiah." In *Uprooting and Planting: Essays on Jeremiah for Leslie Allen*, edited by John Goldingay, 172–189. New York: T & T Clark, 2007.

Hornsby, Theresa. "'Israel has Become a Worthless Thing': Re-Reading Gomer in Hosea 1—3." *JSOT* 24, no. 82 (1999): 115–128.

Hossfeld, Frank-Lothar and Erich Zenger. *A Commentary on Psalms 51–100*. Minneapolis: Fortress, 2005.

Houtman, Cornelis. "The Urim and Thummim: A New Suggestion." *VT* 40, no. 2 (1990): 229–232.

Humphreys, W. Lee. "Where's Sarah? Echoes of a Silent Voice in the 'Akedah'." *Soundings* 81, no. 3–4 (1998): 491–512.

Hurowitz, Victor A. "True Light on the Urim and Thummim." *JQR* 88, no. 3–4 (1998): 263–274.

Jackson, Justin. "The Bows of the Mighty are Broken: The 'Fall' of the Proud and the Exaltation of the Humble in 1 Samuel." *Themelios* 46, no. 2 (2021): 290–305.

Jackson, Melissa A. "Lot's Daughters and Tamar as Tricksters and the Patriarchal Narratives as Feminist Theology." *JSOT* 26, no. 4 (2002): 29–46.

Janzen, J. Gerald. "Prayer and/as Self-Address: The Case of Hannah." In *A God So Near: Essays on Old Testament Theology in Honor of Patrick D. Miller*, edited by Brent A. Strawn and Nancy R. Bowen, 113–127. Winona Lake, IN: Eisenbrauns, 2003.

Jaworski, Adam. *Silence: Interdisciplinary Perspectives*. Berlin: Mouton de Gruyter, 1997.

Jensen, J. Vernon. "Communicative Functions of Silence." *ETC: A Review of General Semantics* 30 (1973): 249–257.

Jeon, Jaeyoung. "The Scout Narrative (Numbers 13) as a Territorial Claim in the Persian Period." *JBL* 139, no. 2 (2020): 255–274.

Jobling, David. "Saul's Fall and Jonathan's Rise: Tradition and Redaction in 1 Sam 14:1–46." *JBL* 95, no. 3 (1976): 367–376.

Johannesen, Richard L. "The Functions of Silence: A Plea for Communication Research." *Western Speech* 38, no. 1 (1974): 25–35.

Jones, Jordan W. "An Embodiment of Silence: The Hand-on-Mouth Gesture in the Hebrew Bible and Ancient Near East." In *The Body: Lived, Cultured, Adorned: Essays on Dress and the Body and Ancient Near East in Honor of Nili S. Fox*, edited by Angela R. Erisman, et al., 49–80. Cincinnati, Ohio: HUC Press, 2022.

Jones, Scott C. "Psalm 37 and the Devotionalization of Instruction in the Postexilic Period." In *Prayers and the Construction of Israelite Identity*, edited by Susanne Gillmayr-Bucher and Maria Häusl, 167–187. Atlanta: SBL, 2019.

Joo, Samantha. "Counter-narratives: Rizpah and the 'Comfort Women' Statue." *JSOT* 44, no. 1 (2019): 79–98.

Kalimi, Isaac. "The Land of Moriah, Mount Moriah, and the Site of Solomon's Temple in Biblical Historiography." *HTR* 83, no. 4 (1990): 345–362.

Kellenberger, Edgar. "Gottes Doppelrolle in Ijob 16." *Bib* 90, no. 2 (2009): 224–236.

Kessler, John. *Between Hearing and Silence: A Study of Old Testament Theology*. Waco, TX: Baylor, 2021.

Kierkegaard, Søren. *Fear and Trembling*. Princeton, NJ: Princeton University Press, 1983.

Kim, Uriah Y. "Uriah the Hittite: A Con(text) of Struggle for Identity." *Semeia* 90–91 (2002): 69–85.

Kitz, Ann Marie. "Effective Simile and Effective Act: Psalm 109, Numbers 5, and KUB 26." *CBQ* 69, no. 3 (2007): 440–456.

Knohl, Israel. "Between Voice and Silence: The Relationship between Prayer and Temple Cult." *JBL* 115, no. 1 (1996): 17–30.

Koenig, Sara M. "Make War Not Love: The Limits of David's Hegemonic Masculinity in 2 Samuel 10–12." *BibInt* 23, no. 4–5 (2015): 489–517.

Korpel, Marjo and Johannes de Moor. *The Silent God*. Leiden: Brill, 2011.

Krisel, William. "Was the Levite's Concubine Unfaithful or Angry? A Proposed Solution to the Text Critical Problem in Judges 19:2." *OTE* 33, no. 3 (2020): 473–489.

Kruger, Paul A. "The Face and Emotions in the Hebrew Bible." *OTE* 18, no. 3 (2005): 651–663.

Kuloba, Wabayanga R. "Athaliah of Judah (2 Kings 11): A Political Anomaly or an Ideological Victim?" In *Looking Through a Glass Bible: Postdisciplinary Biblical Interpretations from the Glasgow School*, edited by A. K. M. Adam and Samuel Tongue, 139–152. Leiden: Brill, 2014.

Kurzon, Dennis. "Towards a Typology of Silence." *Journal of Pragmatics* 39, no. 10 (2007): 1673–1688.

Labuschagne, C. J. "The Metaphor of the So-Called 'Weaned Child' in Psalm cxxxi." *VT* 57, no. 1 (2007): 114–123.

Lambaard, Christo. "Testing Tales: Genesis 22 and Daniel 3 and 6." In *Prayers and the Construction of Israelite Identity*, edited by Susanne Gillmayr-Bucher and Maria Häusl, 113–123. Atlanta: SBL, 2019.

Landy, Francis. "Language and Silence in Isaiah's Oracles Against the Nations." In *Prophetic Otherness: Constructions of Otherness in Prophetic Literature*, edited by Steed V. Davidson and Daniel C. Timmer, 105–125. London: T & T Clark, 2021.

———. "Narrative Techniques and Symbolic Transactions in the Akedah." In *Signs and Wonders: Biblical Texts in Literary Focus*, edited by J. Cheryl Exum, 1–40. Atlanta: SBL, 1989.

Lanser, Susan S. *The Narrative Act: Point of View in Prose Fiction*. Princeton, NJ: Princeton University Press, 1981.

Lasine, Stuart. "Reading Jeroboam's Intentions: Intertextuality, Rhetoric, and History in 1 Kings 12." In *Reading Between Texts: Intertextuality and the Hebrew Bible*, edited by Dana N. Fewell, 133–152. Louisville: Westminster/John Knox, 1992.

Lee, Nancy C. *Lyrics of Lament: From Tragedy to Transformation*. Minneapolis: Fortress, 2010.

Lemos, T. M. "Shame and Mutilation of Enemies in the Hebrew Bible." *JBL* 125, no. 2 (2006): 225–242.

Lenzi, Alan. "Invoking the God: Interpreting Invocations in Mesopotamian Prayers and Biblical Laments of the Individual." *JBL* 129, no. 2 (2010): 303–315.

Leuchter, Mark. "Jeroboam the Ephratite." *JBL* 125, no. 1 (2006): 51–72.

Leveen, Adriane. *Memory and Tradition in the Book of Numbers*. Cambridge: Cambridge University Press, 2008.

Levine, Baruch A. "Silence, Sound, and the Phenomenology of Mourning in Biblical Israel." *JANES* 22 (1993): 89–106.

Linafelt, Tod. "Speech and Silence in the Servant Passages: Towards a Final-Form Reading of the Book of Isaiah." *Koinonia* 5, no. 2 (1993): 174–190.

Lipscomb, Anthony I. " 'They Shall be Clothed in Shame': Is Shame an
    Emotion in the Hebrew Bible?" *Journal of Ancient Judaism* 12, no. 2
    (2021): 313–359.
Lipton, Diana. "Early Mourning? Petitionary Versus Posthumous Ritual in
    Ezekiel XXIV." *VT* 56, no. 2 (2006): 185–202.
Lust, Johan. "A Gentle Breeze or a Roaring Thunderous Sound? Elijah at
    Horeb: 1 Kings XIX 12." *VT* 25, no. 1 (1975): 110–115.
MacCulloch, Diarmaid. *Silence: A Christian History.* New York: Viking, 2013.
MacDonald, Nathan. "Driving a Hard Bargain? Genesis 23 and models of
    Economic Exchange." In *Anthropology and Biblical Studies: Avenues
    of Approach*, edited by Louise J. Lawrence and Mario Aquilar, 79–96.
    Leiden: Deo, 2004.
Magdalene, F. Rachel. "Trying the Crime of Abuse of Royal Authority in
    the Divine Courtroom and the Incident of Naboth's Vineyard." In *The
    Divine Courtroom in Comparative Perspective*, edited by Art Mermeistein
    and Shalom E. Hotz, 167–245. Leiden: Brill, 2015.
Malbon, Elizabeth Struthers, "The Jesus of Mark and the Sea of Galilee," *JBL*
    103, no. 3 (1984): 363–377.
Masullo, Gina M. and Marley Duchovnay. "Extending the Spiral of Silence:
    Theorizing a Typology of Political Self-Silencing." *Communication
    Studies* 73, no. 5–6 (2022): 607–622.
Matthews, Victor H. and Don C. Benjamin. *Old Testament Parallels: Laws
    and Stories from the Ancient Near East*, 5th ed. Mahwah, NJ: Paulist,
    2023.
———. "Amnon and Tamar: A Matter of Honor (2 Samuel 13:1–38)." In
    *Crossing Boundaries and Linking Horizons: Studies in Honor of Michael
    C. Astour*, edited by Gordon D. Young, Mark Chavalas, and Richard E.
    Averbeck, 339–366. Bethesda, MD: CDL Press, 1997.
Matthews, Victor H. *Experiencing Scripture: The Five Senses in Biblical
    Interpretation.* Minneapolis: Fortress, 2023.
———. "The Many Forms and Foundations of Power and Authority in the
    Hebrew Bible." In *T & T Clark Handbook of Anthropology and the
    Hebrew Bible*, edited by Emanuel Pfoh, 189–204. London: T & T Clark,
    2023.
———. "Making Your Point: The Use of Gestures in Ancient Israel." *BTB*
    42, no. 1 (2012): 18–29.
———. *More Than Meets the Ear: Discovering the Hidden Contexts of Old
    Testament Conversations.* Grand Rapids, MI: Eerdmans, 2008.
———. "Messengers and the Transmission of Information in the Mari
    Kingdom," in *Go to the Land I Will Show You: Studies in Honor of*

Dwight W. Young, edited by Victor H. Matthews and Joseph Coleson, 267–274. Winona Lake, IN: Eisenbrauns Publishers, 1996.

———. "Hospitality and Hostility in Genesis 19 and Judges 19." *BTB* 22, no. 1 (1992), 3–11.

———. The King's Call to Justice." *BZ* 35, no. 2 (1991): 204–216.

———. "Theophanies Cultic and Cosmic: 'Prepare to Meet Thy God!'" In *Israel's Apostasy and Restoration: Essays in Honor of Roland K. Harrison*, edited by Avraham Gileadi, 307–317. Grand Rapids, MI: Baker, 1988.

McBride, S. Dean. "Jeremiah and the Levitical Priests of Anathoth." In *Thus Says the Lord: Essays on the Former and Latter Prophets in Honor of Robert R. Wilson*, edited by John J. Ahn and Stephen L. Cook, 179–196. New York: T & T Clark, 2009.

McCarter, R. Kyle. *II Samuel*. New York: Doubleday, 1984.

———. *1 Samuel*. New York: Doubleday, 1980.

McEvenue, Sean. "The Elohist at Work." *ZAW* 96, no. 3 (1984): 315–332.

McKane, William. "Poison, Trial by Ordeal and the Cup of Wrath." *VT* 30, no. 4 (1980): 474–492.

Meadowcroft, Tim. "Who are the Princes of Persia and Greece (Daniel 10)? Pointers Towards the Danielic Vision of Earth and Heaven." *JSOT* 29, no. 1 (2004): 99–113.

Medina, Richard W. "Job's Entrée into a Ritual of Mourning as Seen in the Opening Prose of the Book of Job," *Die Welt des Orients* 38 (2008): 194–202.

Meier, Samuel A. *The Messenger in the Ancient Semitic World*. Atlanta: Scholars Press, 1988.

Mein, Andrew, Else K. Holt, and Hyn Chui Paul Kim, eds. *Concerning the Nations: Essays on The Oracles Against the Nations in Isaiah, Jeremiah, and Ezekiel*. London: Bloomsbury T & T Clark, 2015.

Middleton, J. Richard. *Abraham's Silence: The Binding of Isaac, the Suffering of Job, and How to Talk Back to God*. Grand Rapids, MI: Baker Academic, 2021.

Milgrom, Jacob. *Numbers*. Philadelphia: Jewish Publication Society, 1990.

Miller, Cynthia. "Silence as a Response in Biblical Hebrew Narrative: Strategies of Speakers and Narrators." *JNSL* 32, no. 1 (2006): 23–43.

Milstein, Sara J. "Saul the Levite and His Concubine: The 'Allusive' Quality of Judges 19." *VT* 66, no. 1 (2016): 95–116.

Mirguet, Françoise. "What is an 'Emotion' in the Hebrew Bible: An Experience that Exceeds Most Contemporary Concepts." *BibInt* 24, no. 4–5 (2016): 442–465.

Moore, Michael S. "Bathsheba's Silence (1 Kings 1.11–31)." In *Inspired Speech: Prophecy in the Ancient Near East: Essays in Honor of Herbert B. Huffmon*, edited by John Kaltner and Louis J. Stulman, 336–346. London; New York: T & T Clark, 2004.

Mossman, Judith. *Euripides: Medea*. Oxford: Oxbow, 2010.

Mrozek, Andrzej. "The Motif of the Sleeping Divinity." *CBQ* 80, no. 3 (1999): 415–419.

Muers, Rachel. "Silence and the Patience of God." *Modern Theology* 17, no. 1 (2001): 85–98.

Murphy-O'Connor, Jerome. "Why Doesn't God Answer Prayers? How the First Christians Dealt with Divine Silence," *BRev* 20, no. 2 (2004): 14–19, 43.

Na'aman, Nadav. "The Contest on Mount Carmel (1 Kings 18:19–40) as a Reflection of a Religious-Cultural Threat." *BZ* 64, no. 1 (2020): 85–100.

Naveh, Joseph. "Nameless People." *IEJ* 40, no. 2–3 (1990): 108–123.

Neher, Andre D. "Speech and Silence in Prophecy." *Dor le Dor* 6, no. 2 (1977–78): 61–73.

Ng, Andrew Hock-Soon. "Revisiting Judges 19: a Gothic Perspective." *JSOT* 32, no. 2 (2007): 199–215.

Nichols, Louise A. *Silent Characters in Shakespeare's Plays: Text and Production*. PhD Dissertation; University of Toronto, 1992.

Nicol, George G. "David, Abigail and Bathsheba, Nabal and Uriah: Transformations within a Triangle." *SJOT* 12, no. 1 (1998): 130–145.

———. "The Alleged Rape of Bathsheba: Some Observations on Ambiguity in Biblical Narrative." *JSOT* 22, no. 73 (1997): 43–54.

Noelle-Neumann, Elizabeth. *The Spiral of Silence: Public Opinion—Our Social Skin*, 2nd ed. Chicago: Chicago, 1993.

Noll, K. L. "A Portrait of the Deuteronomistic Historian at Work?" In *Raising Up a Faithful Exegete: Essays in Honor of Richard D. Nelson*, edited by K. L. Noll and Brooks Schramm, 73–86. Winona Lake, IN: Eisenbrauns, 2010.

Noll, Sonja. *The Semantics of Silence in Biblical Hebrew*. London: Brill, 2020.

———. "Rereading Samuel's Silence in 1 Samuel 7:8." *VT* 66, no. 3 (2016): 393–405.

Noort, Ed. "Genesis 22: Human Sacrifice and Theology in the Hebrew Bible." In *The Sacrifice of Isaac: The Aqedah (Genesis 22) and its Interpretations*, edited by Ed Noort and Eibert Tigchelaar, 1–20. Leiden: Brill, 2002.

O'Brien, Mark A. "The Portrayal of Prophets in 2 Kings 2." *Australian Biblical Review* 46 (1998): 1–15.

Olyan, Saul M. *Biblical Mourning: Ritual and Social Dimensions.* Oxford: Oxford, 2004.

———. "Honor, Shame, and Covenant Relations in Ancient Israel and Its Environment," *JBL* 115, no. 2 (1996): 201–218.

Ong, Walter J. *Orality and Literacy.* New York: Routledge, 2002.

Park, Hye Kyung. *Why Not Her? A Form and Literary-Critical Interpretation of the Named and Unnamed Women in the Elijah and Elisha Narratives.* New York: Peter Lang, 2015.

Park, Song-Mi Suzie. "The Frustration of Wisdom: Wisdom, Counsel, and Divine Will in 2 Samuel 17:1–23." *JBL* 128, no. 3 (2009): 453–467.

Park, Wye K. *Why Not Her? A Form and Literary-Critical Interpretation of the Named and Unnamed Women in the Elijah and Elisha Narratives.* New York: Peter Lang, 2015.

Parker, Julie F. "Re-membering the Dismembered: Piecing Together Meaning from Stories of Women and Body Parts in Ancient Near Eastern Literature." *BibInt* 23, no. 2 (2015): 174–190.

Peterson, Brian N. "Another Example of David's Darker Side or a Picture of a Shrewd Monarch?" *JETS* 1, no. 2 (2012): 201–222.

Petrany, Catherine. "Words Fail Me: Silence, Wisdom, and Liturgy in Psalm 73." *Journal of Theological Interpretation* 13, no. 1 (2019): 113–127.

Popitz, Heinrich. *Phenomena of Power: Authority, Domination, and Violence.* New York: Columbia University Press, 2017.

Prochnik, George. *In Pursuit of Silence: Listening for Meaning in a World of Noise.* New York: Doubleday, 2010.

Rabinowitz, Peter J. *Before Reading: Narrative Conventions and the Politics of Interpretation.* Ithaca: Cornel University Press, 1987.

Rainbow, Jesse. "Micaiah be Imlah (1 Kings 22) and the Grammar of the Biblical War Oracle." *JBL* 138, no. 3 (2019): 537–557.

Reames, Robin. "Speech in Pursuit of Silence." *Philosophy & Rhetoric* 55, no. 1 (2022): 32–39

Reinhartz, Adele. "Samson's Mother: An Unnamed Protagonist." In *A Feminist Companion to Judges,* edited by Athalya Brenner, 157–170. Sheffield, England: JSOT Press, 1993.

Reis, Pamela T. "The Levite's Concubine: New Light on a Dark Story." *SJOT* 20, no. 1 (2006): 125–146.

Rembold, Stephanie. "Hannah in Stages and Places: An Exploration of Narrative Space in 1 Samuel 1." *OTE* 35, no. 1 (2022): 68–83.

Rendsburg, Gary. "The Mock of Baal in 1 Kings 18:27." *CBQ* 50, no. 3 (1988): 414–417.

Reymond, Eric D. "The Hebrew Word *damah* and the Root d-m-m ("To be Silent")." *Bib* 90, no. 3 (2009): 374–388.

Rice, Gene. "Elijah's Requirement for Prophetic Leadership (2 Kings 2:1–18)." *Journal of Religious Thought* 59, no. 1 (2006): 1–12.

Robinson, Bernard P. "Elijah at Horeb, 1 Kings 19:1–18: a Coherent Narrative?" *RB* 98, no. 4 (1991): 513–536.

Rogland, Max. "Elijah and the 'Voice' at Horeb (1 Kings 19): Narrative Sequence in the Masoretic Text and Josephus." *VT* 62, no. 1 (2012): 88–94.

Roi, Micha. "The Law of the Sotah and the Cup of Wrath: Substantive and Adjective Law in the Hebrew Bible." *RB* 124, no. 2 (2017): 161–179.

Roncace, Mark. "Elisha and the Woman of Shunem: 2 Kings 4.8–37 and 8:1–6 Read in Conjunction." *JSOT* 25, no. 91 (2000): 109–127.

Routledge, Robin L. "Hosea's Marriage Reconsidered." *TynBul* 69, no. 1 (2018): 25–42.

Rudman, Dominic. "Is the Rabshakeh Also Among the Prophets? A Rhetorical Study of 2 Kings XVIII 17–35." *VT* 50, no. 1 (2000): 100–110.

Russell, Stephen C. "Samuel's Theophany and the Politics of Religious Dreams." In *Perchance to Dream: Dream Divination in the Bible and the Ancient Near East*, edited by Esther Hamori and Jonathan Stökl, 109–132. Atlanta: SBL, 2018.

Sanders, Seth L. "Absalom's Audience (2 Samuel 15–19)." *JBL* 138, no. 3 (2019): 513–536.

Sarna, Nahum. *Genesis*. Philadelphia: Jewish Publication Society, 1989.

Sarot, Marcel. "Deafening Silence? On Hearing God in the Midst of Suffering." In *Reflections on the Silence of God: A Discussion with Marjo Korpel and Johannes de Moor*, edited by Bob Becking, 139–151. Leiden, The Netherlands: Brill, 2013.

Sasson, Jack M. "Oracle Inquiries in Judges." In *Birkat Shalom: Ancient Near Eastern Literature and Postbiblical Judaism Presented to Shalom M. Paul on the Occasion of His Seventieth Birthday*, edited by Chaim Cohen, et al., 149–168. Winona Lake, IN: Eisenbrauns, 2008.

———. "The Blood of Grapes: Viticulture and Intoxication in the Hebrew Bible." In *Drinking in Ancient Societies: History and Culture of Drinks in the Ancient Near East*, edited by Lucio Milano, 399–419. Padua: Sargon, 1994.

Savran, George. "The Time of Her Life: Ruth and Naomi." *Nashim* 30, no. 5777 (2016): 7–23.

Schwatz, Ethan. "The Theological Pretension of the Ethical: Reframing the Jewish Significance of Genesis 22." *Int* 77, no. 1 (2023): 40–51.

Scott, Robert L. "Dialectical Tensions of Speaking and Silence." *Quarterly Journal of Speech* 79, no. 1 (1993): 1–18.

Sergi, Omer. "Saul, David, and the Formation of the Israelite Monarchy." In *Saul, Benjamin, and the Emergence of Monarchy in Israel*, edited by Joachim J. Krause, Omer Sergi, and Kristin Weingart, 57–91. Atlanta: SBL, 2020.

Shamir, Jacob. "Speaking Up and Silencing Out in Face of a Changing Climate of Opinion." *Journalism & Mass Communication Quarterly* 74, no. 3 (1997): 602–614.

Sherwood, Yvonne. "Of Fruit and Corpses and Wordplay Visions: Picturing Amos 8.1–3." *JSOT* 25, no. 92 (2001): 5–27.

Shulman, Ahouva. "Imperative and Second Person Indicative Forms in Biblical Hebrew Prose." *Hebrew Studies* 42 (2001): 271–287.

Sim, David C. "The Man Without the Wedding Garment (Matthew 22:11–13)." *HeyJ* 31, no. 2 (1990): 165–178.

Simmons, J. Aaron. "What About Isaac? Rereading *Fear and Trembling* and Rethinking Kierkegaardian Ethics." *Journal of Religious Ethics* 35, no. 2 (2007): 319–345.

Smith, Gary V. "Amos 5:13: The Deadly Silence of the Prosperous." *JBL* 107, no. 2 (1998): 289–294.

Spieckermann, Hermann. "Schweigen und Beten: von stillen Lobgesang und zerbrechender Rede im Psalter." In *Das Manna fällt auch heute noch Beiträge zur Geschichte und Theologie des Alten Testaments: Festschrift für Erich Zenger*, edited by Frank-Lothar Hossfeld and Ludgar Schwienhorst, 567–584. Freiburg: Herder, 2004.

Spina, Frank A. "A Prophet's 'Pregnant Pause': Samuel's Silence in the Ark Narrative (1 Sam 4:1–7:2)." *Horizons in Biblical Theology* 13, no. 1 (1991): 59–73.

Stiebert, Joanna. "The Body and Voice of God in the Hebrew Bible." *Journal for Religion, Film and Media* 2, no. 1 (2016): 23–33.

Stocks, Simon P. " 'Like the snail that dissolves': Construction of Identity of Psalmist and Enemy in the Lament Psalms of the Individual." *JSOT* 46, no. 1 (20212): 133–143.

Stuhlmueller, Carroll. "Psalm 22: The Deaf and Silent God of Mysticism and Liturgy." *BTB* 12, no. 3 (1982): 86–90.

Sweeney, Marvin A. "A Reassessment of the Masoretic and Septuagint Versions of the Jeroboam Narratives in 1 Kings/3 Kingdoms 11–14." *JSJPHR* 38, no. 2 (2007): 165–195.

Taylor, Marion A. " 'Cold Dead Hands Upon Our Threshold': Josephine Butler's Reading of the Story of the Levite's Concubine, Judges 19–21."

In *The Bible as a Human Witness to Divine Revelation: Hearing the Word of God Through Historically Dissimilar Traditions*, edited by Randall Heskett and Brian P. Irwin, 259–273. New York: T&T Clark, 2010.

Terrien, Samuel. *The Elusive Presence: The Heart of Biblical Theology*. San Francisco: Harper & Row, 1983.

Tigay, Jeffrey H. *Deuteronomy*. Philadelphia: Jewish Publication Society, 1996.

Toker, Leona. *Eloquent Reticence: Withholding Information in Fictional Narrative*. Lexington, KY: University Press of Kentucky, 2014.

Tonstad, Sigve. "The limits of power: Revisiting Elijah and Horeb." *SJOT* 19, no. 2 (2005): 253–266.

Torresan, Paolo. "Silence in the Bible." *JBQ* 31, no. 3 (2003): 153–160.

Trible, Phyllis. *Texts of Terror: Literary-Feminist Readings of Biblical Narrative*. Philadelphia: Fortress, 1984.

Tsfati, Yariv and Shira Dvir-Gvirsman, "Silencing Fellow Citizens: Conceptualization, Measurement, and Validation of a Scale for Measuring the Belief in the Importance of Actively Silencing Others." *International Journal of Public Opinion Research* 30, no. 3 (2018): 391–419.

Turner, Graham. *The Power of Silence: The Riches That Lie Within*. New York: Bloomsbury, 2012.

Urbrock, William J. "The Book of Amos: The Sounds and the Silences." *CurTM* 23, no. 4 (1996): 245–253.

van Dam, Cornelis. *The Urim and Thummim: A Means of Revelation in Ancient Israel*. Winona Lake, IN: Eisenbrauns, 1997.

Van der Horst, Pieter W. "Silent Prayer in Antiquity." *Numen* 41, no. 1 (1994): 1–25.

Vanderkam, James. "David's Complicity in the Deaths of Abner and Eshbaal: A Historical and Redactional Study." *JBL* 99, no. 4 (1980): 521–539.

van Elferen, Isabella and Sven Raeymaekers. "Silent Dark: The Orders of Silence." *Journal for Cultural Research* 19, no. 3 (2015): 262–273.

Van Winkle, D. W. "1 Kings xii 25–xiii 34: Jeroboam's Cultic Innovations and the Man of God from Judah." *VT* 46, no. 1 (1996): 101–114.

van Wolde, Ellen. "A Network of Conventional and Deliberate Metaphors in Psalm 22." *JSOT* 44, no. 4 (2019): 642–666.

Verschueren, Jef. *What People Say They Do with Words*. Northwood, NJ: Ablex, 1985.

Vieira, Monica B. "Representing Silence in Politics." *American Political Science Review* 114, no. 4 (2020): 976–988.

Vijayan, Laila L. "Social Inquisitiveness of Prophetic Imagination and the Silenced Voice of Gomer." *Bangalore Theological Forum* 49, no. 2 (2017): 58–71.

Walsh, Carey, "Under the Influence: Trust and Risk in Biblical Family Drinking," *JSOT* 25, no. 90 (2000): 13–29.

Walters, Stanley D. " 'To the Rock' (2 Samuel 21:10)." *CBQ* 70, no. 3 (2008): 453–464.

Waltman, Joshua C. "Psalms of Lament and God's Silence: Features of Petition Not Yet Answered" *EvQ* 89, no. 2 (2018): 209–221.

Weems, Renita J. "Gomer: Victim of Violence or Victim of Metaphor?" *Semeia* 47 (1989): 87–104.

Weinfeld, Moshe. *Deuteronomy 1–11.* New York: Doubleday, 1991.

Wells, Bruce. "Sex, Lies, and Virginal Rape: The Slandered Bride and False Accusation in Deuteronomy." *JBL* 124, no. 1 (2005): 41–72.

White, Marsha C. "Saul and Jonathan in 1 Samuel 1 and 14." In *Saul in Story and Tradition*, edited by Carl S. Ehrlich, 119–138. Berlin: Mohr Siebeck, 2006.

Williamson, H. G. M. "Sound, Sense, and Language in Isaiah 24–27." *JJS* 46, no. 1–2 (1995): 1–9.

Wöhrle, Jakob. " 'No Future for the Proud Exultant Ones': The Exilic Book of the Four Prophets (Hos., Am., Mic., Zeph.) as a Concept Opposed to the Deuteronomistic History." *VT* 58, no. 4–5 (2008): 608–627.

Wolfers, David. "Reflections on Job xii." *VT* 44, no. 3 (1994): 401–405.

Wong, Gordon C. I. "Faith in the Present Form of Isaiah VII 1–17." *VT* 51, no. 4 (2001): 535–547.

Wong, Gregory T. K. "Ehud and Joab: Separated at Birth?" *VT* 56, no. 3 (2006): 399–412.

Wood, Rebecca. "Foucault, Freda Fry and the Power of Silent Characters on the Radio." In *Gender, Sex, and Gossip in Ambridge: Women in* The Archers, edited by Cara Courage and Nicola Headlam, 77–85. Bingley, England: Emerald Group Publishing, 2019.

Wulf, Christoph. "Präsenz des Schweigens." In *Schweigen: Unterbrechung und Grenze der menschlichen Wirlichkeit*, edited by Dietmar Kamper and Chistoph Wulf, 7–16. Berlin: Reimer, 1992.

Young, Norman H. "The Trial of Jesus before Pilate in the Fourth Gospel: A Comparison with Mark," *EvQ* 92, no. 1 (2021): 1–20.

Zierler, Wendy. "In Search of a Feminist Reading of the Akedah." *NASHIM: A Journal of Jewish Women's Studies and Gender* 9, no. 5765 (2005): 10–26.

Zimran, Yisca. " 'Look, the King Is Weeping and Mourning!': Expressions of Mourning in the David Narratives and Their Interpretative Contribution." *JSOT* 41, no. 4 (2018): 491–517.

SCRIPTURE INDEX

2 Chronicles

3:1	20
32:31	79

Ezra

9:1	78

Nehemiah

5:1-13	50
5:8	50
8:1-12	51
8:10	51
8:11-12	51

Esther

2:1	78
3:1	78
5:1-3	96

Job

1:20-21	99
2:11-13	61
3:3-9	63
4:12-16	70, 115
4:16	115
9:24	64
12:9	64
12:14	57
12:20	57
16:9	88
19:6-12	64
21:5	100

23:10	78
26:5-14	70
29:9	100
32:1	43
32:15	43
37:2-5	68
38:1—39:30	64
40:1—41:34	64
40:4	100
42:1-6	64

Psalms

4:1	62
4:4	64
4:5	57
5:1	61
6:5	62
10	65
13	108
13:1	60, 63
13:3	62
13:5	61
17:3	64
18:13	68
19:1-4	59
19:3	107
20:9	62
22	65, 108, 109
22:1-2	67
22:2	61, 110
22:6-18	109
22:10-11	67
28:1	61, 63, 110
29:3-9	68

Matthew

6:6-7	111
22:12	96
27:13-14	87

Mark

1:25	102
4:25-41	107
4:35-41	116
15:3-5	87

Luke

4:35	102
15:11-19	87
18:37-39	100

John

18:33-38	87

Acts

21:40—22:2	103

1 Corinthians

14:28	106

James

1:19	106

1 Peter

2:15	106

2 Peter

2:7-8	92

Wisdom of Solomon

3:5-6	84

Sirach

20:1	56
20:7	56, 64
26:9	86
27:22	86
46:17	68

Josephus

A.J. 8.13.7 §§349–352

Mishnah

Genesis Rabbah

58:5	22

AUTHOR INDEX